Learning Contentment

Marcus C. Grodi

LEARNING *Contentment*

FINDING PEACE RIGHT WHERE YOU ARE

EWTN Publishing, Inc.
Irondale, Alabama

This volume, previously published by the Coming Home Network International, incorporates material from Marcus Grodi, *Life from Our Land* (Ignatius Press, 2015). This 2025 edition includes minor editorial revisions and two appendices.

Cover design by LUCAS Art & Design, Jenison, MI.

Cover image courtesy of the author.

EWTN Publishing, Inc.
5817 Old Leeds Road, Irondale, AL 35210

Distributed by Sophia Institute Press, Box 5284, Manchester, NH 03108.

paperback ISBN 978-1-68278-451-8
ebook ISBN 978-1-68278-452-5

Library of Congress Control Number: Forthcoming

First printing

CONTENTS

Introduction

One of the most crucially important, yet dagnabittly elusive aspects of not just entering one's "twilight years" but all of adult life is contentment. At least, this has been my experience.

When we wake up and find ourselves in these "twilight years", or are planning ahead for it, we want to be content. We don't want to spend our time looking back with regret, or being anxious about tomorrow, wringing our hands over all the unknowns that keep poking their ugly heads up into our path; or feeling a loss of contentment after all the things upon which our previous contentment seemed to be based are gone. We want to wake up in the morning and, at least after our first or second cup of coffee, look forward with optimistic joy to the day ahead! (The problem I've found over the years, however, with making the morning's first cup of coffee is that I really need to have already had one for it to come out right.)

In his many epistles, Saint Paul often wrote of contentment. When he penned his letter to his Christian friends at Philippi, for example, he happened to be imprisoned and in chains for the preaching of the gospel. After many positive words of encouragement, he wrote:

> Not that I complain of want; for *I have learned, in whatever state I am, to be content.* I know how to be abased, and I know how to abound; in any and all circumstances *I have learned* the

> secret of facing plenty and hunger, abundance and want. I can do all things in him who strengthens me.* (Phil 4:11–13)

What seems important to point out in this profound confession is that Paul doesn't merely say, "I am content in whatever state I am", but rather, "I *have learned to be* content." Whether his life is abased or abounding; whether he's "facing plenty [or] hunger, abundance [or] want", he's "learned the secret" of being content "in any and all circumstances". And to cut to the chase, he concludes by revealing what that secret is, but we'll get to that later.

In other places, he commands his readers not to wait for contentment to sneak up on them as a resultant feeling, but to *choose now to be content*: "[I]f we have food and clothing, with these we shall *be content*" (1 Tim 6:8), and "Keep your life free from the love of money, and be *content* with what you have" (Heb 13:5a).

In yet another place, Paul emphasizes that this contentment, which he exhorts others to choose, is something he himself has chosen: "For the sake of Christ, then, *I am content* with weaknesses, insults, hardships, persecutions, and calamities; for when I am weak, then I am strong" (2 Cor 12:10).

Certainly a feeling of contentment is a joyful and glorious gift. At its core, however, the kind of true, foundational, persistent contentment that Paul speaks of is an attitude we choose; it's a virtue that Paul had to learn, by grace, through "him who strengthens me", as he learned to see the struggles of his life through the lens of the Cross of Christ. Paul even learned to accept the sufferings he received from living the gospel as the means by which he could "complete what is lacking in Christ's afflictions for the sake of his body, that is, the Church" (Col 1:24).

A Brash Act of Discontent

I think Paul would admit that learning contentment is a bit like wisdom or even wine—it matures or ripens with age; it develops

* Throughout this book, any italicized or bolded portions of Scripture or quotes are my own added emphasis.

as we reflect back upon the blessings and mistakes of our past. I can't help but picture Paul, as he sat in his cell encumbered by chains and writing this letter, pausing to remember an event that had happened years before when he first brought the gospel to the Philippian Christians—an event that, with hindsight, he might have handled differently. His companion Luke had recorded it in his *Acts of the Apostles*, so Paul couldn't escape public knowledge of his brash act of discontent.

Paul and Silas, and apparently their new companion Luke, were on their second missionary journey, immediately after the Jerusalem council. They had arrived in Philippi, and on the sabbath, as Paul and his companions were heading toward the synagogue, this is what happened:

> As we were going to the place of prayer, we were met by a slave girl who had a spirit of divination and brought her owners much gain by soothsaying. She followed Paul and us, crying, "These men are servants of the Most High God, who proclaim to you the way of salvation." And this she did for many days.
>
> But Paul was annoyed, and turned and said to the spirit, "I charge you in the name of Jesus Christ to come out of her." And it came out that very hour.
>
> But when her owners saw that their hope of gain was gone, they seized Paul and Silas and dragged them into the market place before the rulers; and when they had brought them to the magistrates they said, "These men are Jews and they are disturbing our city. They advocate customs which it is not lawful for us Romans to accept or practice."
>
> The crowd joined in attacking them; and the magistrates tore the garments off them and gave orders to beat them with rods. And when they had inflicted many blows upon them, they threw them into prison, charging the jailer to keep them safely. Having received this charge, he put them into the inner prison and fastened their feet in the stocks. (Acts 16:16–24)

All because Paul got annoyed. I can just see Silas, as they sat side by side in the stocks, quoting that great philosopher of early-movie fame, Oliver Hardy, saying, "Well, here's another nice mess you've gotten me into." With hindsight, Paul might have wondered if there wasn't maybe a better way he could have handled that. I mean, as crazy as the slave girl might have been, still, she was accurately promoting the spread of the gospel. Maybe with a little more patience or charity, Paul might have avoided their being seized, dragged, convicted, attacked, stripped, beaten with rods, thrown into prison, and stuck in the stocks.

Of course, Paul could claim that the "rest of the story" justified his actions and their sufferings. For, as Luke continues, the benefits that God brought out of this "nice mess" began once they decided to choose contentment:

> But about midnight Paul and Silas were *praying and singing hymns to God*, and the prisoners were listening to them, and suddenly there was a great earthquake, so that the foundations of the prison were shaken; and immediately all the doors were opened and every one's fetters were unfastened. When the jailer woke and saw that the prison doors were open, he drew his sword and was about to kill himself, supposing that the prisoners had escaped.
>
> But Paul cried with a loud voice, "Do not harm yourself, for we are all here."
>
> And [the jailer] called for lights and rushed in, and trembling with fear he fell down before Paul and Silas, and brought them out and said, "Men, what must I do to be saved?"
>
> And they said, "Believe in the Lord Jesus, and you will be saved, you and your household." And they spoke the word of the Lord to him and to all that were in his house.
>
> And [the jailer] took them the same hour of the night, and washed their wounds, and he was baptized at once, with all his family. Then he brought them up into his house, and set food before them; and he rejoiced with all his household that he had believed in God. (Acts 16:25–34)

As Paul reminisced, he may have seen how giving in to discontentment had gotten them into a *nice mess*, whereas an act of grateful, worshipful contentment had opened the floodgates of God's grace and mercy.

As I nudge slowly into these twilight years of retirement, I'm learning to appreciate how much growing in contentment involves looking back and learning from our myriad failures, as well as our victories, which are far more than we deserve, all of which come as a gift of God's mercy and grace.

With this in mind, the following are a few steps that I believe are at least a beginning toward *learning contentment.*

1

Begin Right Where You Are

Never in the history of mankind has the proverbial image comparing society to "frogs in a soup pot" seemed more apropos. You know the old saying about how to cook a frog? If you drop him into a pot of already-boiling water, he'll immediately know it's "too hot for comfort" and jump out. But if you first drop the frog into a pot of body-temperature water, the theory goes, he'll contentedly swim around, not noticing as you gradually raise the temperature, while he cheerfully, though unknowingly, becomes frog soup.

I would suggest that this definitely describes the "soup" we're all living in today, because it seems that the vast majority of us are oblivious to the "rise in temperature" of the world around us. I'm not refering to temperature literally, of course, but to the vociferous voices inundating us with advice on how to live our lives. In the context of this book, I mean the thousands of opinions as to what we need to do, or to change, or to get, or to get rid of, to somehow move a little closer to contentment.

Imagine yourself a frog swimming in an immense soup pot with a thousand other frogs, all croaking at the same time: that's the garrulous guidance coming at us from all sides through today's media. It's tempting to surrender and say, "With such confident croaking, they must know more than I about learning contentment! So, I'll just keep swimming along in this vat with everybody else."

But it's important to remember, "For what will it profit a man, if he gains the whole world"—which is what all those voices want us to strive for—"and forfeits his life?" (Mt 16:26). Maybe the Lord, however, is calling us to do something different—and not just swim against the stream, but maybe even jump out of the pot! Isn't this exactly what our Lord was calling His followers to do, when He said:

> Do not lay up for yourselves treasures on earth … but lay up for yourselves treasures in heaven. … For where your treasure is, there will your heart be also. (Mt 6:19–21)

What kind of treasure are the voices around us in this soup vat encouraging us to lay up? And where is your heart?

I would suggest that our "soup" qualifies as a communal expression of what Saint Ignatius of Loyola once called "desolation" or "spiritual distress." In his *Spiritual Exercises*, Ignatius gave a detailed description of this:

> Spiritual distress: this is the name I give to whatever is opposite to [spiritual comfort or contentment]—darkness of soul, disquiet of mind, an attraction to what is coarse and earthly, all restlessness proceeding from different temptations and disturbances, such as the temptation tending to destroy faith, hope, and charity; the condition in which the soul finds itself listless, apathetic, melancholy, like the one cut off from its Creator and Lord.[1]

I would never presume to delve too deeply into explaining the beautiful depth of Ignatian spirituality, except to admit that what he lists describes much of what I, and so many others, seem to be experiencing at this time in our lives, particularly in the time in which we are living. Does anything on this list describe aspects of your own life?

What Ignatius says next, however, is especially important:

> In a period of distress we are not to alter anything, but should remain firm and unyielding in our resolutions and the purpose

> of mind in which we found ourselves on the day preceding such distress, or in the purpose in which we found ourselves in the preceding comfort. For in times of comfort it is the good spirit that guides us by his counsel, whereas in distress it is the evil spirit; but the latter's counsel will never bring us to a right decision.[2]

I realize there's a lot to unpack here, but we need to appreciate his wisdom and insight: too often people are tempted to make big changes in their lives when they're smack-dab in the midst of great personal distress. Many of us even interpret the presence of these symptoms of distress as the very signs God might be using to call us to make drastic changes. Ignatius warned, however, that this might be the worst time to do this—it might in fact be that God has a particular reason for calling us to remain in our present situation, no matter how seemingly desolate or distressed.

Centuries ago, the prophet Jeremiah wrote a letter to the Israelites who were living through just such a time of desolation. They had been taken into exile, from their beloved home in Jerusalem into Babylon. Certainly, their wish would have been to escape back to Jerusalem, and their hope was that someday soon the Lord would make this possible. In the meantime, however, through the prophet Jeremiah, God gave them a different message:

> Thus says the Lord of hosts, the God of Israel, to all the exiles whom I have sent into exile from Jerusalem to Babylon: Build houses and live in them; plant gardens and eat their produce. Take wives and have sons and daughters; take wives for your sons, and give your daughters in marriage, that they may bear sons and daughters; multiply there, and do not decrease. ***But seek the welfare of the city where I have sent you into exile, and pray to the Lord on its behalf, for in its welfare you will find your welfare.*** (Jer 29:4–7)

After my seventy-plus years of life, I'm pretty sure the life we're living in this crazy, mixed-up twenty-first century can easily be portrayed as an exile of distress. I realize the optimists will all just write me off as a hopeless pessimist, but as I wrote the first draft of this on the morning of the 2024 presidential election, I couldn't help but think that regardless of which party won, we all might just be in for a rough road ahead, as either side fights to prevent the other side from any semblance of success. (I've also heard, as we did in the last few elections, that many Hollywood celebrities are threatening to leave the country if the candidate they abhor gets elected! I'm quite sure that if they do leave, they won't find the contentment they seek, though their absence might just make our contentment a tad more accessible.)

Within the last decade or so, a popular journalist, author, and friend wrote a quite successful book about facing the crazy times in which we live. If my friend happens to read this, I want him to know that I fully agree with most everything he wrote, especially his description of the dire circumstances in which we find ourselves today. His solution was to model our lives after the practices and values of a fifth-century monastic movement. In so many ways I couldn't agree more, but where I differ slightly was his decision to emphasize the formation of like-minded faith communities. His solution for preparing for the coming tribulation was for (small "o") orthodox Christians to establish communities where together they could provide the necessary support for the coming trials.

Certainly, from an idyllic perspective, there's much to say here. Yes, "no man is an island," and sustainable living is close to impossible in isolation. So, wherever and whenever possible, I agree completely that we need to identify like-minded friends with whom we can gain and share mutual support. But the obvious and practical problem with the goal of forming like-minded faith communities is that most of us are already living in circumstances that are not easy to up and vacate. Some of us are living in homes and on property, and in proximity to our jobs, extended family, and friends, that are just not so easy to extricate ourselves from, even if we wanted to.

Regardless of whatever value may come from making a drastic move to abandon all and attempt the experiment of a like-minded community, which would certainly be contrary to the advice of either Saint Ignatius or Jeremiah, this radical move may not bring contentment, and then what? Move to yet another community? What I believe is more urgently important is that we start by seeking the necessary stability for ourselves and our family right now in the place where God has placed us.

If we truly desire peace and fulfillment in this life, it seems to me that the Lord is saying that we must first "seek the welfare" of the place where He has placed us "in exile" and to "pray to the Lord on its behalf, for in its welfare [we] will find [our] welfare." Only by gratefully appreciating and seeking His presence where He has us right now will we experience the blessings where He might call us tomorrow—for I can promise you that the beauty of this rural bed of roses where He has called my family to live has its fair share of thorns, and the biggest thorn for my family to bear is me. Lord, help us.

I think it is also essential that each of us accept the fact that we are living now in this time in history through the wisdom and will of God. It's amazing how many people I know—or whose blogs fill the Internet—who focus so much of their lives on trying to rediscover and live in the past. They look back and see what they consider better and more wholesome ways of living, especially in the pre-industrial era, and then make every effort and sacrifice to return to how life was fifty, one hundred, two hundred, even five hundred years ago. Certainly there is much to praise and emulate in the simpler lives of our pre-industrial ancestors, much of which my own family have tried to implement on our small "cottage farm." But I'm not convinced that the best answer for finding true contentment is to abandon and escape from the very time in which God has called us to live.

I also consider it a dangerous mistake that many of the modern, well-meaning, back-to-the-earth, simple-life, sustainable-farming types want to return to the simpler lifestyle of their grandparents on the farm without the foundation of their grandparents' faith—without their grandparents' vision of recognizing the loving fingerprints of God on everything they possess. Moderns want the simplicity without their grandparents' undergirding faith, philosophy, and sacrifice, and as a result, their goals and decisions are all too often misguided and misdirected.

It's essential to remember that not a one of us was an accident—when and where and to whom we were born was all a mysterious act of God's will. King David the psalmist wrote centuries ago, "Thy eyes beheld my unformed substance; in thy book were written, every one of them, the days that were formed for me, when as yet there was none of them" (Ps 139:16). God reiterated this through the prophet Jeremiah when He said, "Before I formed you in the womb I knew you, and before you were born I consecrated you" (Jer 1:5). Certainly, we can look back and learn what we've lost as our nation, our culture, our world, and our families have surrendered so pervasively to industrialism, materialism, relativism, and rampant selfism. God, however, did not call us to live back then but to take what we have learned from examining the lives of those who have come before us, as well as the plight of our exile, and live it now, by grace, as a faithful and courageous witness to all those around us.

If we are presently in a difficult, dangerous situation, then of course, by all means, we may need to extricate ourselves for both spiritual and physical salvation. But setting these exceptions aside, for the majority of us, during these difficult days, unless we have a clear message from God, confirmed by His chosen representatives, I would suggest we patiently heed Jeremiah's advice. Where God might have us tomorrow is, of course, an unknowable mystery. What we need to accept, though, is that where we are today, right now, no matter how bad or seemingly hopeless, is right in the mysterious hands of God and where we must, first, seek to learn contentment.

Still, I can imagine some demanding, "But are you saying that, to be content, we have to just hunker down and always stay put where we are? Shouldn't a young growing family consider moving to a larger home or a retired couple consider downsizing? Or what if one feels called to change jobs or move his family to a better neighborhood. Is there something wrong with this?"

The simple answer is, "Of course not". Saint Paul wrote that "Abraham believed God, and it was reckoned to him as righteousness" (Rom 4:3). *What* was *it* that was "reckoned to him as righteousness"? He moved! He was willing to trust and obey God's call, to leave his life of contentment in Ur to uproot his family and go to a completely unknown place. He didn't do this because he was discontent and decided he needed to move in the hope of finding contentment; contentment had nothing to do with it. Abraham trusted God and obeyed, which was the foundation for Saint Paul's understanding of his own radical call to leave his life of contentment as a Jewish Pharisee to become a missionary in this strange new sect called *The Way*—"to bring about the obedience of faith" (Rom 1:5).

Saints Anthony of the Desert and Francis of Assisi didn't abandon their comfortable, contented wealthy lives with the primary goal of seeking contentment—though this is, in fact, what they found. They did this in obedience to the Lord's call to become perfect: "If you would be perfect, go, sell what you possess and give to the poor, and you will have treasure in heaven; and come follow me" (Mt 19:21).

All I'm recommending, for now, in line with the advice of Saint Ignatius, is that before making any drastic changes, seek to understand God's call to true contentment first right where you are. Then you can be more certain that your thoughts about making a radical change are not driven by a false hope of finding contentment elsewhere.

Allow me to add one more thing. We need to begin learning contentment not just right where we are but by being content with the person we see every morning when we look in the mirror. It's truly disturbing how pervasive the voices in our lives insist that we'll never be content until we become someone different than who we are. We look in the mirror and see someone who needs to be thinner or heavier, taller or shorter, less wrinkled with more or different colored hair, et cetera, et cetera. Some of us avoid mirrors altogether—at least until after that first cup or two of morning coffee—because the sight is just too depressing.

Regardless of what changes we think we need to make, or actually do need to make for the sake of our health, still, I believe it is essential that we begin by learning contentment with the person we see in the mirror right now. That is the person whom God created in His image; that is the person whom God so loved that He sent His Son; and that is the person whom God still loves so much that there is nothing in all of creation that can separate us from His love in Christ Jesus (cf. Rom 8:31–39). My hope is that by the end of this book, the steps I'm suggesting will help you make decisions for the right reasons for the future of yourself and your family.

I have always found the words of Psalm 121 comforting. This psalm was the confession of a man who had lost his way; who had been drawn away from the people of God into the desolation of pagan rituals. By God's mercy, however, he eventually found his way home:

> I [lifted] up my eyes to the hills. From whence [did] my help come? My help [came] from the Lord, who made heaven and earth. He will not let your foot be moved, he who keeps you will not slumber. Behold, he who keeps Israel will neither slumber nor sleep. The Lord is your keeper; the Lord is your shade on your right hand. The sun shall not smite you by day, nor the moon by night. The Lord will keep you from all evil; he will keep your life. The Lord will keep your going out and your coming in from this time forth and for evermore.[3]

All that follows in this book are words of encouragement on how to learn and choose, by the grace of God, true contentment. To do this doesn't require first changing where we live, or who we are, or getting a better or different job, or changing our relationships. All of this may come, but learning and experiencing true contentment needs to begin right now, today, in seeking the welfare of the place and situation in which God has placed us right now, "for in its welfare you will find your welfare."

2

LOVE THE ONE YOU'RE WITH

"Love the one you're with": I'm hesitant to quote this line from the controversial post-Woodstock rock hit written by Stephen Stills, but this is exactly the point I want to make, as a continuation of the last chapter. Certainly, given the same exceptions mentioned, there may be situations in which the only path toward contentment is to extricate oneself from a destructive, demoralizing, even dangerous relationship. But other than any necessary exceptions, choosing contentment does not necessitate changing relationships, especially in the most permanent of relationships, marriage. We need to accept that where we are today, right now, no matter how bad or seemingly hopeless, is right in the mysterious hands of God.

Several times our Lord affirmed that the second-greatest commandment is that we are to love one another as we love ourselves. This seemingly self-focused criterion actually connects with the Golden Rule: we are to love others as we wish they would love us. So, given the possibility that some of us reading this (as well as writing this) aren't always the most loving or lovable people on earth, learning contentment requires choosing contentment with the others in our lives as we hope they will choose contentment in their relationships with us. Our contentment must not be contingent upon their actions or attitudes; rather, we are to learn and choose contentment in spite of, even sometimes in reaction to, all the specifics in our day-by-day relationships. And again, this most importantly refers to those of us who are married.

So, what do I need to do, beginning right now, to be the best husband, father, and grandfather I can be, by grace, for the rest of my life? There's an important twist in my focus here: the question is not just how I am to learn contentment in my marriage, but what do *I* need to do to make it easier for my loving wife, Marilyn, to experience contentment in this marriage of ours?

Let me begin with a disclaimer: I'm not going to presume to prescribe anything new in this chapter, partially because I know that many of you reading this have superior experiential credentials for answering these questions than I have.

But as I look back just over my seventy-plus years of life, and thirty-nine years of marriage, it's truly disturbing how our culture's view of marriage, family, sexuality, and morality has changed—and I am certain our parents and especially our grandparents could never have imagined the drastic views being pushed by a wide swath of our population. And we and our marriages—and our children's marriages—are right now all in this "soup."

So the one question I want to focus on in this chapter is what can we do to make sure that our marriages don't just survive but become overflowing with love, joy, and peace, so that they become natural seedbeds of contentment for both our wives and ourselves?

The second thing I need to state as I begin this chapter is that I am primarily speaking to husbands. I think most of what I'll be saying applies equally to us all, husband or wife, but I don't consider myself worthy to give advice to you ladies. I'm just speaking to you guys.

I also recognize that I have not earned the right to speak above you as some kind of expert; at best, I'm speaking beside you. I'm not presuming to tell you anything; I just want to talk with you about how we can be better husbands, fathers, and grandfathers, so that in our learning and choosing of contentment, we can help our wives to also grow in contentment.

Ephesians 5

For this, I'd like to first look at Saint Paul's discussion of marriage in Ephesians 5:25–33a. On the one hand, this comes from one of the most well-known sections in Scripture on marriage. On the other, however, it's one of the more controversial. But I'm only going to examine the husband's side of Paul's recommendations (and leave Paul's instructions to wives for you ladies to read at your leisure):[4]

> Husbands, love your wives, as Christ loved the church and gave himself up for her, that he might sanctify her, having cleansed her by the washing of water with the word, that he might present the church to himself in splendor, without spot or wrinkle or any such thing, that she might be holy and without blemish. Even so husbands should love their wives as their own bodies. He who loves his wife loves himself. For no man ever hates his own flesh, but nourishes and cherishes it, as Christ does the church, because we are members of his body. "For this reason a man shall leave his father and mother and be joined to his wife, and the two shall become one flesh." This mystery is a profound one, and I am saying that it refers to Christ and the church; however, let each one of you love his wife as himself.

In this section of Ephesians, there are surrounding verses where Paul speaks directly to wives. However, Paul was not telling husbands, "Hey, look at what your wife is supposed to do—and make sure she does it!" Rather, he was telling husbands to focus on what *we* are supposed to do—regardless of what our wives do.

And what are we to do? *We are to love our wives as Christ loves the Church.*

This is one of the reasons why the first thing we see when we enter a church is a cross or a crucifix, to remind us of how we are to love our wives: *That's* how. In essence, this is saying that we are to give ourselves completely to the task of presenting our wives to Christ holy and blameless.

1 Peter 3

There's a parallel verse by Saint Peter in his first letter, but from a slightly different angle. After first speaking to wives, he turns his attention to us husbands:

> Likewise you husbands, live considerately with your wives, bestowing honor on [them], since you are joint heirs of the grace of life, in order that your prayers may not be hindered. (1 Ptr 3:7)

Three things come quickly from this text. First, Peter calls husbands to "live considerately with your wives." That's our ongoing challenge, to live considerately. And what does this mean? Maybe it means doing all we can to make it easier for her to learn and choose contentment while she puts up with our "few" shortcomings?

As I entered my retirement years, I encountered a new and significant challenge. All of our kids are gone, and now my wife, Marilyn, and I are to live alone, out in our "cabin in the woods." Also, because my days are no longer spent from nine to five away at the office, or traveling, I will be spending most of my time at home, on what has been for decades her turf, her daily kingdom. So, in a new way and in a new context, we're learning to "live considerately" with one another. And the person facing the biggest challenge is not me.

Second, Peter says that we husbands are "to bestow honor" on our wives, since we "are joint heirs of the grace of life." Through the sacrament of marriage, we have become one. In mostly quoting Scripture, the Catholic *Catechism* teaches:

> Holy Scripture affirms that man and woman were created for one another: "It is not good that the man should be alone" (Gen 2:18). … "Therefore a man leaves his father and his mother and cleaves to his wife, and they become one flesh" (Gen 2:14). The Lord himself shows that this signifies an unbreakable union of their two lives by recalling what the plan of the Creator had been "in the beginning": "So they are no longer two, but one flesh" (Mt 19:6).[5]

Whether we feel like it or not, we have become, in a mysterious yet significant sense, truly united as One. From the moment we said, "I do," all of our thoughts and plans needed to evolve—to no longer think only about what *I* need to do but what *we*, my wife and I, need to do; no longer what's best for *me* but what's best for *us*; and no longer what *I* need to do to avoid hell and make it into heaven but what do *we* need to do. Actually, our job, husbands, to apply Paul's earlier advice, is to give completely of ourselves so that by grace we can sanctify our wives, that we might present her to Christ in splendor, without spot or wrinkle or any such thing, that she might be holy and without blemish.

Thirdly, Saint Peter says that we need to live considerately with our other half "in order that [our] prayers may not be hindered." Ever wonder, guys, what's standing in the way, spiritually, from your growing closer to God? Do your prayers sometimes seem like they're bouncing off the walls of heaven? Is it possibly because we're not living as loving, caring, and considerately with our wives as we ought?

In other words, both Paul and Peter are telling us husbands—are telling me—that our primary goal needs to be to help our wives grow in grace and contentment, and in the process, this will open the doors so that we, too, can have the best chance of growing ourselves in grace and contentment.

Galatians 5:22–23

Thirty-nine-plus years ago, when Marilyn and I picked out our wedding bands, we had engraved on the inside of each ring a reference to a favorite Scripture text, one that I've always considered crucial, not only to life in Christ but especially for a successful marriage. The problem is that it would be nearly impossible to prove this to you because I'd need a hefty pair of tin snips to get this ring off my fat ring finger to show you the engraving—which is also ironic, because the hidden engraving hardly serves as any kind of reminder. It was a good thought, though. The engraved reference was *Galatians 5:22–23*, which reads:

> But the fruit of the Spirit is love, joy, peace, patience, kindness, goodness, faithfulness, gentleness, self-control.

Marilyn and I realized when we began our marriage that to achieve any level of marital contentment, we would have to be *loving*; we wanted a *joyful* and *peaceful* marriage; we knew we needed to be *patient* and *kind* with one another; we wanted our family to be full of *goodness*; we wanted to be *faithful* with each other in every way; we wanted to learn to be *gentle* with each other; and we knew for all of that we would need *self-control*. Consequently, we both knew, knowing ourselves as we did upon entering into this great challenge, that we drastically needed help!

This is precisely what Paul was saying in this text: not that we are expected to do these things for each other on our own strength but that they are "fruit of the Spirit."

To address this, I want to consider two additional portions of Scripture from both Peter and Paul. As you saw earlier, both saints wrote advice directly related to marriage. In these additional texts, however, they more generally discuss how you and I are to *abide* in Christ, to *continue* in Him, and to live out our baptismal faith, which forms the foundation for understanding the necessity of the *fruit of the Spirit* in our marriages.

Galatians 5:16–17

The first of these comes from Paul's *Letter to the Galatians*:

> But I say, *walk by the Spirit*, and do not gratify the desires of the flesh. For the desires of the flesh are against the Spirit, and the desires of the Spirit are against the flesh; for these are opposed to each other, to prevent you from doing what you would. (Gal 5:16–17)

To understand the significance of this, it's important to remember a few things. First, remember that Paul said, in 2 Corinthians 5:17, that "if any one is in Christ, he is an new creation; the old has passed away, behold the new has come." This may not be true for you, but sometimes I forget that because of our faith in Christ and through baptism—because of the sacraments—we have been changed. Regardless of whether we feel it or even act like it, if by faith and through baptism, we are in Christ, we are new creations; the old has gone, the new has come; we are children of God; we are part of the Mystical Body of Christ; and through our reception of the sacraments of baptism and confirmation, we have received the gifts of the Spirit, like seeds of holiness waiting to sprout, to come alive.

Part of the problem, though, is that we forget all this, especially the gifts and our need to act on them, which is why Paul said that, even though by faith and baptism we have *received* the Holy Spirit, who abides within us, we are still called to "***walk*** by the Spirit." His command is that we willfully "walk by the Spirit," who dwells within us. At the same time, we are to willfully refuse to "gratify the desires of the flesh." Here Paul addresses the battle that rages in every one of us, in every human being: a battle of the desires, the desires of the flesh versus the desire of the Spirit, and these, as he said, "are opposed to each other, to prevent you from doing what you would."

He also addressed the mystery of God's providence and mercy. By grace, God changes us through faith and baptism, yet in His love, He also lets us go, giving us the freedom to respond to Him and His love. We are not puppets. God never forces anyone to love or obey Him, or to love one another. He calls us to do this freely.

In the context of marriage, especially today, there is a spiritual battle raging to prevent our marriages from succeeding. Much of this battle comes from the world around us, but the most difficult battle rages within each of us; within the consciences of both halves of a married couple. Which is why to experience the fruit of the Spirit in marriage, we both need to willfully and prayerfully walk by the indwelling Spirit.

2 Peter 1

Saint Peter also said this in a most profound way, but as you read this, I want you to remember that if by faith and baptism you are in Christ, then Peter is speaking to *you*—what he is saying is true of *you*:

> His divine power has granted to us all things that pertain to life and godliness, through the knowledge of him who called

> us to his own glory and excellence, by which he has granted to us his precious and very great promises, that through these you may escape from the corruption that is in the world because of passion, and *become partakers of the divine nature.* (2 Ptr 1:3–4)

When Peter points to "the corruption that is in the world because of passion," does this not sound like he's pointing directly at the world in which we now live? And particularly that the corruption that is running so rampant in our world and culture, and frankly ruining so many thousands of marriages, is "because of passion"? This is why "His divine power"—the indwelling Holy Spirit and His gifts—has been given to us so that we can escape this onslaught of corruption and therefore "become partakers of the divine nature."

This is not a Gnostic battle between the spirit and the flesh, as if only our spiritual nature is good and our fleshly bodies are bad, such that salvation means freeing our spirit from this corrupt, earthly body. Rather, both Paul and Peter speak about the spiritual battle that is in each one of us, between the desires of our lower nature, our sinful self, and the desires of our new self, re-created by faith and baptism in the Spirit.

The New Testament writers emphasized, though, that the evidence of this inner battle in each of us is shown in our actions. In other words, the temptations we have, the desires, the passions, will show themselves in our character, in what we do, what we say, and how we live out our Christian convictions.

Galatians 5:19–21

Paul continued in his letter to the Galatians with a list of the kinds of actions that we must choose to avoid:

> Now the *works of the flesh* are plain: fornication, impurity, licentiousness, idolatry, sorcery, enmity, strife, jealousy, anger, selfishness, dissension, party spirit, envy, drunkenness, carousing, and the like. I warn you, as I warned you before, that *those*

> *who do such things shall not inherit the kingdom of God.* (Gal 5:19–21)

For those of you my age, doesn't this list sound a bit like a candid description of our free-for-all college days back in the early seventies? Well, it seems to me that this is also exponentially true of the world we hear about every night on the evening news.

The vices that Paul lists first and then last may seem so obviously wrong that our eyes may gloss over the rest, causing us to presume we've skirted through this list without guilt. The vices in the middle of this list, however, may hit closer to home, though we still may not take them as seriously as we should: "strife, jealousy, anger, selfishness, dissension." As opposed to the other, more obviously wrong vices, these are the more common ways in which we are tempted to live differently from how we are called to live in Christ, and therefore they deserve to be included in those actions that can prevent us from inheriting the kingdom of God.

This is a very important warning, one that is far too often ignored, not just by the general public who presume that "everyone who dies just goes to a better place" but also by Christians who merely presume that attending church once in a while, taking part in the sacraments, reciting the Creed and liturgical prayers, putting a little bit in the plate, and being a fairly decent person are sufficient for us to one day just "pass on to a better place."

What's so important to recognize, however, like the "frog in the pot" analogy I mentioned earlier, is that we live today in a culture that no longer recognizes the actions in this list as "vices." A disconcerting majority of those pushing "woke" ideologies endorse lifestyles redolent with "fornication, impurity, licentiousness, idolatry, sorcery … party spirit, envy, drunkenness, carousing, and the like," and this sounds disturbingly similar to a warning Paul once gave to his understudy, Saint Timothy:

> But understand this, that in the last days there will come times of stress. For men will be lovers of self, lovers of money, proud,

> arrogant, abusive, disobedient to their parents, ungrateful, unholy, inhuman, implacable, slanderers, profligates, fierce, haters of good, treacherous, reckless, swollen with conceit, lovers of pleasure rather than lovers of God, holding the form of religion but denying the power of it. Avoid such people. (2 Tim 3:1–5)

With this quote I'm not insisting that "it's the end of the world," but Paul certainly seems to be describing our present world, especially in the last phase: "holding the form of religion but denying the power of it."

At this point, I need to remind us of what Paul also wrote to the Christian believers at Corinth:

> For we must all appear before the judgment seat of Christ, so that each one may receive good or evil, *according to what he has done in the body.* (2 Cor 5:10)

Our actions in this life—what we do in and with our bodies—express how well, by grace, we are living by faith and fighting the inner battle of our desires.

I consider it significant that Paul parallels the "*works* of the flesh" not with "*works* of the Spirit" but with the "*fruit* of the Spirit," as listed earlier. The point is that when you or I succumb to temptation and do the "works of the flesh," that's our fault, and we are culpable—and one day, maybe soon, we'll stand accountable before God. If, on the other hand, we resist these temptations and act more in line with the desires of Christ, we are to gratefully recognize these actions as the work of His grace and love in our lives.

Those of you my age may remember a comedian on television who used to claim, whenever he failed, that "the devil made me do it!" No. The devil can't make us do anything; he may tempt us, but always in the end, it's our choice. Whenever we fail, we have no one to blame but ourselves.

When it comes to growing in the virtues described as the "fruit of the Spirit," we are called to recognize that this isn't exactly you or me; it is the work of the Holy Spirit, awakening, convicting, empowering, and encouraging us to want to be different. And I need to say here that this is also true of our learning and choosing contentment: it's the mysterious work of the Holy Spirit, awakening, convicting, empowering, and encouraging, yet also giving us the freedom to choose.

This mystery is expressed in the fact that while here Paul calls these virtues the "fruit of the Spirit," we can all think of many Scriptures throughout the New Testament where we are called to act on these virtues. For example, here Paul calls "love" a fruit of the Spirit, but we can recall many verses where we are commanded to love—to love God and to love one another, "our neighbor as ourselves," even our enemies! Paul calls "joy" a fruit of the Spirit, but elsewhere he says we are called to "*rejoice* in the Lord always" (Phil 4:4). In the same verse, Paul says "peace" is a fruit, but elsewhere he says, "Strive for peace with all men" (Heb 12:14).

This all reiterates that in Christ we are in partnership with the Holy Spirit. When we received the Holy Spirit and His gifts, we didn't automatically start acting or feeling like a different person; we were called to freely actualize the gifts we'd been given. This is why throughout the New Testament we find verses commanding Christians to act on these virtues—here we find the mystery between the work of God in our lives and our own actions in response to grace. As mentioned earlier, when we receive the fruits of the Spirit, they are like seeds of holiness waiting to sprout, but for this to happen, we must act on these gifts.

2 Peter 1:5–11

This is expressed clearly by Peter in his second letter, 1:5–7:

> For this very reason make every effort
> to supplement your faith with virtue,
> and virtue with knowledge,
> and knowledge with self-control,
> and self-control with steadfastness,

> and steadfastness with godliness,
> and godliness with brotherly affection,
> and brotherly affection with love.

Here Peter clearly emphasizes that conversion, as well as growing in contentment, is a process in which we are to make every effort to bring the fruit of the Spirit alive in our lives. Contrary to what so many Christians believe and preach, faith *alone* is never sufficient for our salvation, nor are baptism and the rest of the sacraments sufficient; rather, *faith* includes actively affirming and acting on the existence of God's grace and the fruit in our lives. If we want the fruit of the Spirit to be present in our marriages, then we need to "make every effort," empowered by grace, to be loving, to be joyful, to work for peace, to be patient, to be kind, to insist on goodness, to be faithful, to be gentle, and to exercise self-control.

These two saintly apostles and New Testament authors both emphasize how important it is to walk by the Spirit. In his second letter, Peter writes:

> For if these things are yours and abound, they keep you from being ineffective or unfruitful in the knowledge of our Lord Jesus Christ. For whoever lacks these things is blind and short-sighted and has forgotten that he was cleansed from his old sins. (2 Ptr 1:8–10)

Paul adds, after his list of fruit of the Spirit:

> And those who belong to Christ Jesus have crucified the flesh with its passions and desires. *If we live by the Spirit, let us also walk by the Spirit.* (Gal 5:24,25)

If we've been reborn through faith and baptism, empowered through confirmation, forgiven and cleansed through the sacrament of reconciliation, enriched through the sacrament of the Eucharist, and united as one in the sacrament of marriage, we, therefore, are living by the Spirit. For this to make a difference in our lives, however, and in our marriages, we must walk by the Spirit.

Maybe Peter adds the best conclusion to this:

> Therefore, brethren, be the more zealous to confirm your call and election, for if you do this you will never fall; so there will be richly provided for you an entrance into the eternal kingdom of our Lord and Savior Jesus Christ. (2 Ptr 1:11)

Growing in Marital Contentment

So, how does this all apply to growing in marital contentment? I began this chapter with the following quote from Peter: "Husbands, live considerately with your wives, bestowing honor on [them], since you are joint heirs of the grace of life, in order that your prayers may not be hindered." What can we do to ensure that our marriages are not destroyed by the onslaught of the desires of the flesh, the attacks of the evil one, and the screaming voices of our culture that are trying to redefine marriage, as well as sexuality and personhood?

First, I need to point out that all of these verses emphasize how we are to walk side by side, together, walking by the Spirit, who changes both husband and wife together. This is one of the reasons Paul warned the early Christians not to be unequally yoked. There's a well-known illustration, long used by Christian premarital counselors, that explains how a husband and wife will grow closer together to the extent that they both grow closer to Christ. Unfortunately, the opposite is also true: If one partner makes every effort to grow closer to Christ, to actualize the virtues, while the other partner doesn't, it's very likely they may grow farther and farther apart. If by grace, however, we have been awakened to the need for our marriages to be filled with the fruit of the Spirit as described by Paul, we must not wait for our other half to get on board with these things. Actually, guys, it's probably more often than not that it's our wives who are waiting for us to get on board.

So, guys, the really first place for us to begin is *prayer*. In his letter to the Philippians, Paul wrote a powerful passage about prayer that also involves both the gifts of the Spirit and our parallel acting upon them:

> *Rejoice* in the Lord always; again I will say, *Rejoice*. Let all men know your forbearance. The Lord is at hand. Have no anxiety about anything, but in everything by *prayer and supplication with thanksgiving* let your requests be made known to God. And the *peace of God*, which passes all understanding, will keep your hearts and your minds in Christ Jesus. (Phil 4:4–7)

To *rejoice* means to choose *joy*, even in the midst of anxiety; this involves actively presenting every aspect of our lives to God in prayer—and *supplication with thanksgiving* means grounding every request we make of God upon the foundation of thanksgiving, or as it's often quipped, through the "attitude of gratitude." If we do this, by grace, Paul promised that we will experience the fruit of peace.

However, guys, the problem may be that we still feel that our prayers are going nowhere; we may feel like we're not talking to anyone, or that no one seems to be listening. With this, it's good to remember what Peter warned: that our prayers may be hindered because we're not living considerately with our wives. Maybe we're far more "content" about the present condition of our marriage than we ought to be.

Sounds kind of like we're back to square one. Which is why the best thing we can do for our marriages, right now, today, is, as the two most revered apostles Peter and Paul said, to make every effort to supplement our faith with these virtues—for the sake of our marriages, for the sake of our wives, to show our love for our wives by being these things by grace. Today, pray for God to give you the grace to:

- Love your wife as Christ loved the Church and gave himself up for her;
- Live considerately with her, bestowing honor on her

- Rejoice in the Lord always for her and with her;
- Establish peace in your marriage and home (which may require beginning with an apology);
- Be patient and kind;
- Exemplify goodness, faithfulness, gentleness, and self-control;
- Supplement all these with steadfastness and godliness;
- And always choose contentment, as Saint Paul says, "in whatever state" you are.

3

Focus on the Stable & Established

Often, discontentment arises from the stress of living in the *soup* of the accelerating instability of our progressive culture. I would suggest that we need to rip ourselves free from the grasp of this demon and turn our focus onto that which is stable and established.

In 1776, during the American Revolution, Thomas Paine published his famous phrase "These are the times that try men's souls." I think many people would agree that today's times might be at least as, if not exponentially more, trying to our souls than those of Paine, given how immediate our worldwide digital media has made the increasing chaos in our own nation, culture, and world.

I have heard far more than a few express their desire to escape the trials and tribulations of the city, for the peace and safety of the rural countryside—as they presume my family and I have done. Admittedly, one of the original reasons for our move to this rural setting may have been this escape, and from where you sit, things may look and sound far more promising out where we live. In this difficult time, however, many are tempted to make more than just radical changes in where they live. Many are second-guessing their vocations, occupations, relationships, even their very biological identities. The obsessive desire to change and choose freely seems to have escalated into an irreversible chaos. Is this not all just a desperate search for contentment?

As I look back just on my own lifetime, I'm truly amazed at how fast things are changing in our lives and world. Take, for example, the *great advancements in communication* throughout the history of mankind. Mankind went for centuries with only verbal or hand communications and scratching out symbols on rocks. Long-distance communication required either yelling more loudly and waving more emphatically, sending out messengers ("apostles"), or passing around dried-mud cuneiform tablets. Then someone invented papyrus and paper and chalk and ink and quills and binding, but still, for centuries distant communication was limited to screaming, messengers, and hand-copying.

Then movable type came along, and printing, and mass publishing, and then fountain pens, typewriters, telegraphs, telephones, loudspeakers, radio, television, computers, cell phones, Internet, email, texting, smartphones, social networking, et cetera, et cetera, et cetera, and you get my drift. Note the acceleration of these advancements, or should I just say, changes, in how we communicate. Now, with every single day bringing some new communications advancement and product, it hardly pays to buy anything new because by tomorrow it will be obsolete. We have no way of identifying or predicting the goal of this progress in communications. *We are living on the accelerating trajectory of a communications revolution that has no foreseeable destination.*

Take, for another example, the *history of travel*. For many centuries, men traveled on foot; then came the use of critters, then the wheel, then carriages, chariots, and wagons. These improvements carried men for centuries, until the industrial age brought the bicycle, the steamship, the train, the automobile, the motorcycle, and then the airplane, and space travel, and the Segway Personal Transporter, self-driving electric cars, and on and on (I'll not mention clowns on unicycles).

What is significant is that the acceleration of these advancements has reached such a breakneck speed that we really have no way of projecting where travel will be in fifty years, twenty, five, or even one year from now. Nor can we identify the goal of this progress in transportation. *We are living on the accelerating trajectory of a travel revolution that has no foreseeable destination.*

This same historical accelerating phenomenon is true of nearly every aspect of our lives: trade, information, markets, clothing styles, goods and services, medical care and insurance, and particularly *change* itself. There was a time when people lived their entire lives with few changes in any of these things: from the time they were born until they died, they barely saw changes in clothing, communication, travel, cuisine, or even politics.

Today we live on the vertiginous trajectory of change in everything, and the anxiety of trying to live in this accelerating, goalless culture of presumed progress is also accelerating—and this includes the acceleration of crime and drugs, divorce and broken lives, even the increase in the previously unimagined acceptance of immoral lifestyles, as well as the increase in suicides and interest in euthanasia.

Significantly, this also parallels the rise in our national, global, and personal debt and, interestingly, the historic rise in persecution and martyrdoms—or just cancelations— of those who try to stand for what has always been known as right, true, and beautiful. This all parallels the increasing challenges to our religious freedom in this "land of the free and home of the brave."

Some today are so enamored of—or dare I say, addicted to—the ever-increasing enticements of our modern, industrial, progressivist culture that their answer is to view this accelerating, ever-changing and ever-precarious, economic culture as the inevitable trajectory of human ingenuity—human evolution—and, therefore, a thrilling blessing that must be freely embraced. They see no reason to question any of the demands of this culture; rather, they preach that we are to trust our futures to the trajectory of progress.

Others are not so sure. In a recent interview with the *Los Angeles Times*, Denis Villeneuve, director of the sci-fi franchise, *Dune*, spoke strongly about his fears of how these technologies are affecting our lives and culture, saying:

> [H]uman beings are ruled by algorithms right now. … We behave like *AI* circuits. The ways we see the world are

> narrow-minded binaries. We're disconnecting from each other, and society is crumbling in some ways. It's frightening. ... There's something addictive about the fact that you can access any information, any song, any book. It's compulsive. It's like a drug. I'm very tempted to disconnect myself. It would be fresh air.[6]

All of these vertiginous trajectories of change in everything parallel the seeming exponential decrease of contentment amongst every level of our population. And for so many, their excuse for unwarranted, even irrational change is a desperate search for some toehold on contentment.

When we're riding the ever-changing wave of economic progress, we can become dangerously and falsely contented by the sight of thousands of others mindlessly riding along beside us. They coax us along, assuring us that there is nothing to fear ahead: "Surely economic growth and human ingenuity will prevail in the end, and, of course, doesn't God bless the *faithful*?"

In His *Sermon on the Mount*, however, our Lord Jesus told His followers that true contentment comes through a radically different process, by turning our focus away from the anxieties of our lives and onto, of all things, "the birds of the air" and "the lilies of the field." At first hearing, this sounds absurd. I would suggest, however, that it makes more sense to make every effort to untie our lives from the unrelenting grip of our ever-changing world and, instead, to tie our lives and those of our families to that which is stable and never changing, to that which has been here from the beginning and will always be here, at least until our Lord returns to replace it with a new heaven and a new earth.

Certainly, as baptized Christians, we are no longer citizens of this world, but mere sojourners, pilgrims here, passing through (see Jn 17:14, 16). Jesus, however, did not take us immediately out of this world but left us here to be witnesses to the truth (Jn 17:15). This world, which is our God-given way station on our journey towards our permanent home, was created good and for our enjoyment, as well as our sustenance. As Saint James wrote:

> Every good endowment and every perfect gift is from above, coming down from the Father of lights with whom there is no variation or shadow due to change. (James 1:17)

When we pause to look into the night sky, we should consider that, with the naked eye, regardless of the accelerating changes around us, the stars have not changed in their positions in the constellations since they were created in love by our Father God. The stars were in their precise locations for every person who has ever lived (even given the profound findings and theories of astronomical science).

I recall vividly one night, as I crossed the yard from the house out to the chicken house to shut the clucks in, glancing up at the clear night sky. *Ursa Major* was up to my left, and further up to my right shone *Jupiter*. Scientific materialists will use every means available to study the stars, their origins and compositions, using technology to get us closer and closer to them, but never in their lifetime, in a generation of lifetimes, will they discover the beauty and purpose of the stars and other celestial objects until they recognize that behind it all is the love of our Creator God for the highest in His creation, Man.

When young shepherd David sat on a hillside three thousand years ago tending his sheep, gazing upon *Ursa Major* and *Jupiter*, these gifts in the sky were doing the same thing that they should be doing for you and me today: drawing our thankful hearts upward to our loving Creator God. In awe, David wrote these words:

> When I look at thy heavens, the work of thy fingers,
> the moon and the stars which thou hast established;
> what is man that thou art mindful of him,
> and the son of man that thou dost care for him?
> Yet thou hast made him little less than God,
> and dost crown him with glory and honor.
> Thou hast given him dominion over the works of thy hands;
> thou hast put all things under his feet,
> all sheep and oxen,

and also the beasts of the field,
the birds of the air, and the fish of the sea,
whatever passes along the paths of the sea.
O LORD, our LORD,
how majestic is thy name in all the earth! (Ps 8:3–9)

One can also detect this stability through the patient study of nature and wildlife. With the constant, ever-escalating changes around us, throughout history, through the rise and fall of cultures, empires, and civilizations, the animals and plants continue on, seemingly undaunted by any of this. Certainly, their lives and existence, sometimes even their genetic compositions, are affected by our care or neglect, our conservation or exploitation, yet God has granted them freedom from intellectual questions or concern. This is why God has given us the responsible stewardship of their needs. The chipmunks that feast off the spilled grain in my barn live out their lives in the stability and balance of nature—dare I say contentment—as their ancestors have done for hundreds of generations.

An even more powerful yet intimate means of growing in appreciation of that which is stable and established is to contemplate the mere flame of a candle. The most common object in nearly every religious sanctuary around the world is a candle, and the flames that burn during worship on the wicks of these candles have not changed since the creation of the world.

In the privacy of your "prayer closet," light a candle, and watch, choosing contentment in the midst of everything else that might be pressing down upon you. Anything else you might place before you in some way has been altered by man or beast, shaped, compounded, extruded, purged, or polluted, even a fistful of dirt, but this simple flame has always remained the same. It flickers and moves, as it consumes the wax and responds to the air in the room, even to one's motions, yet this mysterious flicker—but a spark of all the fires raging around the world—is a connection with all the people who have ever warmed themselves, or cooked, read, worshipped, or fellowshipped around a fire throughout history. It unites us with the stable and established, and it unites us with our Creator: "The Lord is my light and my salvation, whom shall I fear?" (Ps 27:1a).

This step gives us a solid handhold for the steps that follow.

4

Recognize That He's Clearly Here

Years ago, I dabbled for a time in scientific materialism. I have always loved science, which shaped my high school and collegiate studies, and my years in industry. During my college years, I abandoned my childhood faith, accepting the possibility that all of life can be explained through biology, physics, chemistry, and mathematics; that the seemingly infinite diversity of nature can be simply explained through mutations, natural selection, and survival of the fittest, all given the miraculous ingredient of enough time.

My journey back to God, however, began not in a worship service, a Bible study, or a revival meeting but, of all places, a genetics class. We were studying the evolutionary development of our senses of sight and hearing. The professor was exhorting us, holding his biology text high like an evangelist holding forth his Bible, to recognize with excitement how these amazing senses had just happened by chance over millions of years through mutation and natural selection. He then elevated before us, as if a holy talisman, a large model of the human eye. It was at this moment that the Holy Spirit used this pseudo-religious ritual to spark a few neuron synapses in my brain: "Wait a second, how could this be true? Does anyone really believe this? The majority of all higher-level living creatures have two eyes at essentially the same location in the front of their heads: Is this merely by chance? Did this arrangement happen over time as a result of natural selection? Is there any fossil evidence showing humanoids or other animals with eyes at less advantageous locations on their bodies, on the back of their heads or rumps?" It struck me that for most of the evolutionists I was studying under, their God was Time; in other words, given enough time and probability, everything could be explained. All order was a mere chance result of millions of years of natural selection. Facing the absurdity of this was what drew me back from chaotic, dead-end thinking to God.

Yet another seemingly insignificant thing that helped me see the inadequacies of the evolutionary, natural-selection mindset was the miracle of birds—not just their seemingly effortless, mesmerizing ability to fly but particularly the fact that nearly every bird species has its own unique song. Consider, for example, that every single Prothonotary Warbler in the world not only has the exact same shape and colorings but the same unique song. For hundreds of years, ornithologists have distinguished bird species not just by their physical characteristics but by each species' unique call—the phrase of sounds that each bird repeats. Some try to explain this through Darwinian evolution, genetics, natural selection, and the survival of the fittest, but I could not see how any of this clearly explains why and how every individual bird of a species around the world has the same song. All beagles may have similar-sounding barks, but they don't all retort the same exact series of barks (e.g., two short low barks, then one long high bark, followed by a growl) every time they open their mouths.

Through pious and humble reflection, this and other astounding facts in nature led me—and can lead any person who by grace is willing to "stop, look, and listen"—to appreciate gratefully the creative love of God, who from the beginning of time, established His symphony of song in nature. Do you hear it? Do you stand in awe? Or do you ignore the miracle and merely jump into your car and, behind closed, tinted windows, speed off to work or your kid's soccer field?

Through His teachings, Jesus encouraged His followers to look around at creation for evidence of our Heavenly Father's existence, love, and care. In our Lord's *Sermon on the Mount*, He said, "Look at the birds of the air; they neither sow nor reap nor gather into barns, and yet your heavenly Father feeds them. Are you not of more value than they?" (Mt 6:26). In another place, Jesus made a similar comparison: "Are not five sparrows sold for two pennies? And not one of them is forgotten before God. Why, even the hairs of your head are all numbered. Fear not; you are of more value than many sparrows" (Lk 12:6–7). Jesus assumed His audience recognized the beauty, order, and care of God in the lives of mere birds—but had they extrapolated from this the care of God in their own lives?

Great spiritual writers throughout the ages have likewise used nature as the starting point to prove God's existence and His intimacy. For example, Saint Bonaventure, the prolific thirteenth-century Franciscan philosopher, in his *Journey of the Mind to God*, gave six steps toward achieving intimacy with God. The first step involves looking at the vestiges (or visible evidence) of God in His creation and recognizing the beauty, order, variety, et cetera as signs of His creative love. This was not a new insight by the great Franciscan philosopher but merely a reflection on what had always been clearly proclaimed in Scripture.

King David, for example, opened one of his most famous psalms with the following affirmation, not of something new but of that which he assumed his audience already believed:

> The heavens are telling the glory of God;
> and the firmament proclaims his handiwork.
> Day to day pours forth speech,
> and night to night declares knowledge.
> There is no speech, nor are there words;
> their voice is not heard;
> yet their voice goes out through all the earth,
> and their words to the end of the world.
> (Ps 19:1–4)

Centuries later, the Apostle Paul, building on this common assumption, wrote to the Roman Christians:

> Ever since the creation of the world [God's] invisible nature, namely, his eternal power and deity, has been clearly perceived in the things that have been made. So they are without excuse, for although they knew God they did not honor him as God or give thanks to him, but they became futile in their thinking and their senseless minds were darkened. Claiming to be wise, they became fools, and exchanged the glory of the immortal God for images resembling mortal man or birds or animals or reptiles. (Rom 1:20–23)

About 125 years later, in AD 175, Saint Irenaeus, the bishop of Lyons in what is now France, wrote a monumental book entitled *Against Heresies*. There is far too much to say, in this short chapter, about this important early Christian work, by a writer who has recently been declared a Doctor of the Church, other than to note that nearly all Christian scholars and historians—Catholic, Protestant, or Eastern Orthodox—agree that Irenaeus was a disciple of Saint Polycarp, who himself was a disciple of Saint John the Apostle, a disciple of Jesus Christ. In other words, Irenaeus was a third-generation direct witness to the gospel of Jesus Christ.

He was moved to write his large book, issued as five separate books as he was able to complete them, because already these third-generation Christians were being inundated by false gospels, promulgated by sometimes very charismatic preachers who, in the name of Christ, were teaching heresy. Irenaeus dedicated a long portion of his life to writing this book with the goal of helping the Christians under his charge know what was true so that they could faithfully follow Christ and be assured of what was necessary for their salvation.

In *Book Two*, after describing in detail the primary gnostic teachers and their often-outlandish philosophies, Irenaeus points out that even they had to explain the evidence of God in the witness of creation. Seeming to expound on Paul's earlier statement from Romans, he wrote:

> Now, that God is the Artificer [Fabricator] of the world, themselves also hold, who in many ways contradict Him, yet confess

> Him, calling him Artificer [Fabricator] … all men in effect agreeing herein: first the ancients, both keeping especially this persuasion by tradition from the first-made Man, and honoring with hymns One God, Maker of Heaven and Earth, then the rest who came after them, receiving from God's Prophets the commemoration of the same: and lastly, the Gentiles learning it from the Creation itself. *For the Creation of itself points to Him Who created it, and the thing made gives intimation of Him Who made it, and the world manifests Him Who set it in order.* Moreover, the whole Church in all the world has received this tradition of the Apostles.[7]

David, Paul, Irenaeus, Bonaventure, and countless others have witnessed to the evidence of God in the stable and established world around us, but let's jump forward to a more modern witness. Dr. A.J. Cronin was once one of the most popular and distinguished twentieth-century novelists in the English-speaking world, best known for *The Citadel* and *The Keys of the Kingdom*, a memorable story of a Catholic missionary in China. He was also renowned as a key voice in the renewal of medical practice in the British Isles. Though raised as a Catholic in Scotland, he drifted into agnosticism during his medical studies. Looking back, he later admitted, as a young medical student, "I was no different than the others of the breed. In the anatomy rooms, dissecting formalin-impregnated remains, the human body seemed to me no more than a complex machine. None of the autopsies showed anything I could identify with an immortal soul. When I thought of God, it was with a superior smile, indicative of biological scorn for such an outworn myth."[8]

It was through the regular practice of his profession, however, visiting patients throughout the valleys of South Wales, assisting at the miracle of birth and the bedside of death, but mainly through observing "the courage and good humor of my fellow-creatures struggling under great hardship" that he "penetrated into the realm of the spirit."[9]

Eventually when he composed an account of his conversion back to faith, he wrote:

> If we consider the physical universe, in its mystery and wonder, its order and intricacy, its awe-inspiring immensity, we cannot escape the notion of a primary Creator. Who on a still summer night dare gaze upward at the stars, glittering in infinity, without the overpowering conviction that such a cosmos came to being through something more than blind indeterminate chance? And our own world, whirling through space in measured rhythm, unfolding its regular progression of the seasons, surely is more than a meaningless ball of matter, thrown off by the merest accident from the sun?
>
> Reject if you will as pure imagery the Biblical presentation of God, shaping the world with His own hands in six days. Smile—should you feel disposed—at Michelangelo's bearded patriarchal figure in the Sistine chapel—prototype of that God the Creator whom men of humble faith accepted in the past—sending the spark of life from His finger into Adam. Accept evolution with its fossils and elementary species, its scientific doctrine of natural causes. And still you are confronted with the same mystery, primary and profound. *Ex nihilo nihil*, as the Latin tag of our school days has it: nothing can come of nothing. …
>
> The truth is, in all the investigations of science into the nature and purpose of these tremendous awe-inspiring processes, these processes stretching backward into the incalculable abysses of time, and of which we can have no more than a fleeting glimpse, there is no valid basis for denying the existence of God. Rather is one driven to conclude that in primordial creation, in the motivation of the universe and the operation of the natural laws there is, has been and always will be a Supreme Intelligence.[10]

This topic is very important and personal to me. In fact, at age seventy-three, I'm literally amazed daily by the clear witness of creation to its Creator. And I know that the foundation of whatever contentment I have attained is built and buttressed by the grateful realization that this world—and my life itself—were purposefully created by a loving, merciful God.

I certainly can't force you to see this; no one can. But God's people have always recognized that the evidence of God's love and His creative actions are clearly evident in the creation around us—if we are willing to look and see.

5

Reduce the Incessant Voices

One of the most frustrating road-bumps to attaining any of the things I've mentioned so far is that our lives are inundated with contrary voices exhorting us to do otherwise. This is why we need to examine and subsequently reduce the incessant voices in our lives. What are we reading? To whom are we listening? Whom are we following on social media? What books, magazines, television shows, radio commentators, news broadcasts, blogs, Internet pundits, and social media "influencers" fill our every waking moment? Are they pulling us closer to God and true contentment, or enticing us to sell our souls along the accelerating path of economic progress and wealth? Are they encouraging us to trust our futures to the "certain" earnings of our investments, or are they helping us to see that the more we detach ourselves from these vaporous promises, and their slant on the world, the freer we are to enjoy the blessings of the present moment—to "have no anxiety about anything" (Phil. 4:6)?

A well-known comedian once described the crisis he caused in his family when he listened to the radio broadcast of "The Chicken Heart That Ate Up New York City." His parents had left him home alone in his crib (a different time, a different world). Against his father's specific orders, he snuck out of his crib and turned on the scary classic radio program *Lights Out*. Once he had become totally terrified by the loud thumping chicken heart, which the narrator said was coming down his street and was now standing outside his door, he spread Jello everywhere to slip up that monster! When his parents returned, hearing the loud thumping of the radio chicken heart, his father screamed, slipped, and nearly killed himself. When he asked his son what the @#$%& was going on, the frightened child screamed in terror, "The chicken heart's coming to eat us up!" His father's solution? He turned the radio off! In the sudden, still silence of their home, the young child admitted sheepishly, "I never thought of that."

How many of the voices in our lives do we merely need to turn off to make true progress towards the stability and peace that God promises? Dorothy Day said it well eighty-plus years ago in her journal:

> "Turn off your radio, put away your daily paper. Read one review of events a week and spend time reading." Life would go on; other people would continue to "eat, sleep, love, worship, marry, have children, and somehow live in the midst of war, in the midst of anguish." Herself, she would pray, work, and read novels.[11]

I remember, years ago now, driving through a pleasant small village in central Ohio. At the one central stoplight, I pulled to a stop. The intersection was a beautifully preserved portrait of nostalgic rural America. Across the way, in a small, immaculately tended park honoring the town's Civil War veterans, a grove of two-hundred-year-old maples and oaks were afire in fall foliage. Under their bows, a teenage girl passed. She walked briskly, face down, earbuds implanted, her attention solely on the smartphone in her hands, her fingers working intently in textual conversation with someone not there. She reached the corner, glanced up just long enough to see the confirmation of the lighted man on the crosswalk sign, then regained her gait and returned to her conversation. She continued across the intersection, up onto the next curb, and then out of my sight. She had not noticed or demonstrated any concern for anything around her. When I was young, in those innocent days before earbuds, Walkmans®, or even transistor radios, I would have had little to distract me from those surroundings. I may have been kicking a can or chucking a stone, but I'm sure I would have been at least a little curious, maybe even a bit observant of the park, the statue of the Union soldier, the cascading red leaves, and the squirrels scurrying frantically in preparation for winter. But this modern teenage girl wasn't really *there*; she was miles away, and the park and its symbols were inconsequential.

The economist E.F. Schumacher is best known for his seminal work, *Small Is Beautiful.*[12] Much of what he wrote and believed is applicable to almost everything I'm trying to say in this book. I'd like to draw attention, though, to an article he wrote in 1976, five years after his conversion to the Catholic faith, entitled, "Technology & Political Change." He wrote:

> As our modern society is unquestionably in crisis, there must be something that does not fit: (a) If overall performance is poor despite brilliant technology, maybe the "system" does not fit. (b) Or maybe the technology itself does not fit present-day realities, including human nature. … I never cease to be astonished at the docility with which people—even those who call themselves Socialists or Marxists—accept technology, uncritically, as if technology were a part of Natural Law.[13]

In other words, for centuries people have blamed the problems in the world on the governmental and political systems, whether communist, socialist, Marxist, Republican, Democratic, capitalist, libertarian, et cetera, while always presuming that the rising technologies in all these systems were good and beyond blame.

He continued:

> People still say: it is not the technology; it is the "system". Maybe a particular "system" gave birth to this technology; but now it stares us in the face that the system we have is the product, the inevitable product, of the technology. As I compare the societies which appear to have different "systems", the evidence

> seems to be overwhelming that where they employ the same technology they act very much the same and become more alike every day. Mindless work in office or factory is equally mindless under any system.
>
> I suggest therefore that those who want to promote a better society, achieve a better system, must not confine their activities to attempts to change the "superstructure"—laws, rules, agreements, taxes, welfare, education, health services, etc. The expenditure incurred in trying to buy a better society can be like pouring money into a bottomless pit. If there is no change in the base—which is technology—there is unlikely to be any real change in the superstructure.[14]

What I consider particularly astounding about these comments is that they were said long before our modern lives had become so irrevocably entrenched in addictive technologies. In 1976, when Schumacher made what were then bold comments, there were no personal or laptop computers; no cell or smartphones; no iPads, iPods, or even Walkmans® (which were not released until 1978); no cable or satellite television; no email or texting; no social networks; no Nintendos, Xboxes, or PlayStations®; there were none of these technologies that demand our regular subscriptions, upgrades, syncing, and constant attention.

Back in 1976, if Schumacher had unplugged his landline telephone or left his home, he would have been living in a world where he was essentially unreachable, and free. Can you imagine being anywhere without your cell phone? Can any of us go a month, a week, or even a day without any of these addictive technologies? The question is, are we better and holier people with these technologies, or because of them? Has our culture become more wholesome and godly through the growth of these technologies? Or is it the system, politics, ideologies, and superstructure of our culture that is the problem? Schumacher would say it isn't the system—it is the technologies that have enticed, captured, and carried us away.

I'm not here just condemning all technology as evil. Heck, I'd be an absurd hypocrite to suggest ridding our lives completely of technology. I mean, seriously, I'm using an iMac right now to edit this book that I wrote on an assortment of computers, and your ability to read this has required countless forms of advanced technologies. Ever try to use any of the everyday tools of yesteryear? Ever try to cut down a tree with a two-man crosscut saw rather than a chainsaw? Ever try to dig a ditch with a shovel rather than a tractor and backhoe? Ever try to go back to handwriting a diary after only using a computer for ten-plus years? I know from experience that it's nearly impossible to go back because the necessary muscles have either atrophied or never developed. I believe this is also true for the spiritual, emotional, and mental muscles of our culture. Generally, when we try to simplify our lives, we give up quickly, because it requires far more effort than we're either willing or able to give.

On the contrary, I believe every technology ever developed by Man, from the wheel up to the most recent digital breakthroughs, was originally given by God to awaken Mankind to His love and ever-present providential care; every technology was given because God "desires all men to be saved and to come to the knowledge of the truth" (see 1 Tim 2:4). God wants you and me to *know* Him. Even technology only given to lessen Man's load or to enhance his enjoyment of life was intended to draw him to his knees in gratitude. The problem is that from the beginning, the world, the flesh, and the devil have done everything possible to skew Man's use of technology toward every other purpose except the deeper knowledge of its source. Mankind proudly pats itself on the back rather than thanks God for His selfless generosity.

I'm just saying that choosing to grow in true contentment means using some common sense to make sure we ourselves control the influence of technology, and its influencers, in our lives, rather than being in their control. As someone wisely quipped: "Technology is a great slave, but a terrible master." We need to silence those earbuds as we walk through nature, so we can appreciate the magnificent beauty, as well as the inspiring symphony of the crickets and birds. And we need to silence—if not at least selectively limit—the noise from "books, magazines, television shows, radio commentators, news broadcasts, blogs, Internet pundits, and social media 'influencers,'" so we can hear God's voice as we walk through this challenging world.

There's another voice, however, that is even more pervasive and nefarious, whispering in the ears of the world's population, though most in the world would deny its presence, and that's the voice of the Tempter. One of his most prevalent strategies, especially in our modern post-Christian age, is certainly the simple goal of just convincing everyone that he and his demonic hoard do not exist. This has had the effect of allowing the devil and his hoard increasing and pervasive, unbounded freedom.

One of C.S. Lewis' most popular books remains his *Screwtape Letters*, which collects a series of imaginative instructions, from a senior demon, Screwtape, to his underling demon, Wormwood. In this, the senior demon is shepherding his novice demon on how to most effectively tempt and turn his human victim away from "the Enemy," who from their perspective is God. In their correspondence, Wormwood has supposedly asked Screwtape "whether it is essential to keep the patient in ignorance of [our] existence." Screwtape answers:

> That question, at least for the present phase of the struggle, has been answered for us by the High Command. Our policy, for the moment, is to conceal ourselves. … I do not think you will have much difficulty in keeping the patient in the dark. The fact that "devils" are predominantly comic figures in the modern imagination will help you. If any faint suspicion of your existence begins to arise in his mind, suggest to him a picture of something in red tights, and persuade him that since he cannot believe in that (it is an old textbook method of confusing them) he therefore cannot believe in you. (39–40)

Just curious: if the idea of the devil ever passes swiftly through your mind, do you possibly see him in a red suit with horns, a long, pointed tail, and a three-pronged pitchfork? That's the image that has always come to my mind, ever since I wore just such a costume as a boy haunting the neighborhood one Halloween. I think this had a lasting influence in keeping me from taking the devil's existence and influence seriously in my own life, until by grace as an adult I was starkly awakened to reality.

6

Live More Simply

This is going to be the longest chapter of this book, not only because, when it comes to learning and choosing contentment, I consider it the most crucial but because I consider it the most needed and neglected today—I believe it addresses the most ignored aspect of our Lord's gospel of the kingdom.

I am hardly the first voice in the past two thousand years of Christianity to suggest that a life in the footsteps of Christ is a life of simplicity. This has been the constant message of the Church and the saints, as well as spiritual writers throughout the ages, ever since our Lord made this the centerpiece of His New Law, His *Sermon on the Mount*. So, to that extent, I hardly need to reiterate this, except maybe to emphasize that this is always a relative move—relative to a person's present state of life and to where he is at the present moment: Are our goals or objectives, our labor, plans, investments, and dreams all leading away from or toward a life of simplicity? Or are they in complicity with our culture, driven by self-promotion, consumption, accumulation, and hoarding?

Early on, the Apostle Paul warned his congregations to beware of the constant call away from the pure, simple gospel of Christ:

> But I fear, lest by any means, as the serpent beguiled Eve through his subtlety, so your minds should be corrupted from the simplicity that is in Christ. (2 Cor 11:3, KJV)

Indeed, the voices of temptation bombarding us from every direction, originating from the age-long battle of the enemy against simplicity, are very subtle, and they have always been gradual and subtle, relying on the means and technologies of each age. Today, however, the call away from simplicity towards progress is at such an accelerating pace that the mere suggestion of choosing a simpler life is a dangerous clarion cry of treason against our American right of upward mobility and the pursuit of the "American dream."

I can still sense many complaining about such uncalled-for attacks on the technologies that have become so pervasive and necessary in our twenty-first-century lives. But Jesus made a far bolder attack on the lifestyles of His first-century audience:

> If your right eye causes you to sin, pluck it out and throw it away; it is better that you lose one of your members than that your whole body be thrown into hell. And if your right hand causes you to sin, cut it off and throw it away; it is better that you lose one of your members than that your whole body go into hell. (Mt 5:29–30)

Why would Jesus make such brash statements to those He was trying to attract as disciples? He was using hyperbole to drive home to His audience how serious He was about the central issue in all His teaching:

> You, therefore, must be perfect, as your heavenly Father is perfect. (Mt 5:48)

Theologians throughout the ages have tried to simplify, clarify, justify, soften, even belittle, explain away, or merely ignore this statement, but the bottom line, as emphasized later by Paul, is that we are called to be holy:

> Since we have these promises, beloved, let us cleanse ourselves from every defilement of body and spirit, and make holiness perfect in the fear of God. (2 Cor 7:1)

If Jesus emphasized that what we do with our hands and what we look at with our eyes are crucial to our growth in holiness, and consequently our relationship with Him, shouldn't we be just as vigilant now with what we hold in our hands, put before our eyes, or plug into our ears?

Every step we make, even small ones, to simplify our lives—to examine critically how addicted we have become especially to communicative technologies—is an effort to get in step with our Lord. Every step in rebellion against the marketeers who claim that happiness and contentment come only with the accumulation of more and more stuff, and against the politicians who warn that the salvation of our economy and the "world as we know it" depends upon this, is a step of freedom from the frantic clutches of today's modern, industrial, progressivist culture.

Earlier I suggested that a life of simplicity is relative to a person's present state of life and to where he is at the present moment. If we desire to simplify our lives, and take a step back to behold the ever-towering hoard of material goods that overflow our present lives, where and how do we begin? Actually, philosophers and theologians, as well as Jesus and His apostles, have long addressed this, calling us to recognize that all material goods are not equal. Some are necessary to our well-being, while others aren't. Making this distinction seems to be a wisdom quite lacking in our modern culture, when we look at the "stuff" that fills our neighbors' houses—never our own, of course! Ever notice how the junk our neighbors try to get rid of through a garage sale—in an attempt to simplify their lives—becomes another neighbor's treasure?

The Apostle Paul referred to this philosophical distinction when he wrote:

> ***[I]f we have food and clothing, with these we shall be content.*** But those who desire to be rich fall into temptation, into a snare, into many senseless and hurtful desires that plunge men into ruin and destruction. For the love of money is the root of all evils; it is through this craving that some have wandered away from the faith and pierced their hearts with many pangs. (1 Tim 6:8–10)

On the one hand are necessary material goods, like food and clothing, while on the other is the pursuit of unnecessary, even deleterious goods, accumulated, collected, even hoarded by "those who desire to be rich," for isn't this what being "rich" generally means?

A very helpful way to understand this was expressed by the great philosopher Saint Thomas Aquinas, as explained by George Speltz, in his dissertation, *The Importance of the Rural Life, According to the Philosophy of Saint Thomas Aquinas.*[15] Aquinas began with the assumption that "an adequate provision of material goods is necessary for the practice of virtue."[16] In other words, it's difficult to focus on cleaning up our spiritual lives—our souls—if the needs of our body are not being met. On the other hand, as Paul says above, if our basic bodily needs are met, he even suggests that with this alone we came learn to be content.

Speltz goes on to explain Saint Thomas Aquinas' theory of the hierarchy of material goods:

> The Thomistic synthesis [pegs] material goods into a fixed place within the hierarchy of man's need. This is achieved in part, by relegating them as means to an end that is outside and above them, to an end that is fixed and capable of controlling them. …
>
> [Material] goods that pertain to the conservation of an individual, i.e., those that are immediately ordered to a fundamental need of the body, as food and drink, are called goods of the body (*bonum corporis*); those that are not ordered in a general way to human needs, fall into the class of external goods (*bonum exterius*). Such are riches (*divitiae*). Of these two classes of material goods, those called "bodily goods" are the higher because necessary for the practice of virtue.[17]

All material goods in this world are instrumental means to the ends for which they were created. Material goods are not ends in themselves. In our sinfulness, however, we human beings can become inordinately preoccupied with them as ends for which we dedicate our time, talents, and money to accumulate, even to hoard.

Not all material goods are equal instruments because the ends for which they were created are not equal: the highest goods, of course, are those that unite us with God ("divine goods"); the second highest are those that nurture our souls; the third highest are "bodily goods" that provide for the needs of the body (food, drink, clothing, shelter), which enable us to reach for the higher goods; and the lowest are the rest, external goods: they do not naturally unite us with God, nurture our souls, or provide for our bodily needs.

This is one of the many mistakes of the modern "health and wealth gospel" preachers. They don't merely promise the neces sary bodily goods but point to the acquisition and accumulation of external lesser goods as the "sure sign of God's blessing." Certainly, God can use anything by grace to bring us to Him. He can indeed shower us with material goods, but we have to be cautious in assuming this is a "sure sign of God's blessing"—it may be a test of our faithfulness, or a temptation from the enemy to turn away from trusting in God's providence. We must beware of using this as an excuse for accumulating lesser material goods.

Speltz continues:

> The amount of [bodily goods] necessary for the practice of virtue, and consequently for [contentment], is strictly limited, a truth emphasized both by Aristotle and by Aquinas. On the other hand, external goods, namely riches, inasmuch as they are ordered only in a general manner to human needs, are not regarded as essential for "an act of virtue." Since riches are sought for their power to procure other things rather than for the direct satisfaction of some bodily need, they easily come to be desired inordinately. ... As a result of this inordinate desire for riches, man is unduly preoccupied with the quest for material goods, failing to realize, as Saint Thomas points out, that riches are the least among human goods.[18]

In this is an amazing and important point: essentially, "bodily goods" are self-regulating, whereas "exterior goods" are not. Normally we can eat just so much, drink just so much, wear just so many clothes, and need just so much shelter. Theoretically, a person can determine how much he needs to eat or drink in a day, a week, a month, and a year, and consequently plan, procure, and store this. A person can also determine what kind of clothes she needs to meet the demands of the climate in which she lives and plan, procure, and store this. And a person can determine how much he needs to shelter himself and his family, then build and maintain it. Certainly, our concupiscence can lead us to be gluttonous and crave more food, drink, clothing, and shelter than we need, like the man in the Gospels who tore down his old barns to build new ones, but still, we always can compare what we have, or want to have, to what we really need.

With the lesser "exterior goods," however, there is no inherent need, so essentially anything at all is over and above what we "need." Certainly, God has created and allowed these external goods for our enjoyment. However, as lesser goods with no inherent limitation, they can be desired inordinately. Our concupiscence can convince us that we "need" these things—to "keep up with the Joneses" or to sustain our reputation in the community, in our work, even in our church, or just because we have more than enough money to provide for our bodily needs. With no obvious need level, there is no limit to the amount of material goods we can justify for ourselves, and we can become so attached to them that we can become convinced we cannot live without them.

Speltz explains how Aquinas used this topic to express his elevated view of the common, simple farmer of his day, the "husbandman":

> Since the need of any one household for natural wealth, such as food and clothing, is limited, so also the activity of the husbandman, as long as it was directed to the procuring of the bodily goods and not of external goods primarily, was proportionately limited and tended less to become inordinate. It was comparatively easy in the agrarian way of life advocated by Aristotle and Aquinas, for the people to retain a true evaluation of

> bodily goods, as opposed to external goods, the former having a fixed relation to the needs of the various households.[19]

In other words, when most families lived in a rural setting, in small communities where generally everyone was content with producing sufficient bodily goods, a farmer's work and life were also, therefore, limited. Though farm work was hard and physically demanding, the farmer knew when his work was done. He could relax contented once he had done all that was necessary that day to provide for the bodily needs of his family. As long as they lived untouched by the obsession of the outside world for lesser material goods, the simple contented farm family could live happily, content with the food, drink, clothing, and shelter they needed and gratefully assumed God had provided, and the spiritual enrichment of their local parish.

However, when the simplicity of the rural farm family was shattered by the lure of the city, when farm children were lured away to work in factories, or to train in colleges for leadership roles in industry, trading houses, or investment firms, not for the procurement of more bodily goods or spiritual enrichment, but "for wealth and what it will buy,"[20] their lives became limitlessly driven. Or, as the post–World War I song taunted, "How Ya Gonna Keep 'Em Down on the Farm, after They've Seen Paree?"[21]

Even the natural limits of bodily goods became shattered. Today, when does one ever have enough specialty foods, flavored cappuccinos, designer clothing, and suburban sprawl homes, not to mention electronics, cars, toys, books, CDs, DVDs, video games, and money? When can anyone sit back and relax content that they have produced and accumulated all the bodily and material goods they will ever need? When have we reached our "number" to know we have invested enough in our 401Ks to provide all the goods we will need to keep us "in the lifestyle to which we have become accustomed" until we die—which today is being extended longer, longer, and longer.

All technologies that underlie all occupations at their core emerge from the gifts that God planted in His creation and, to varying degrees, especially guided by grace, can lead to the production and nurture of the higher goods. As I said earlier, I believe every technology ever developed by Man was originally given to awaken Mankind to God's love and ever-present providential care. However, because technology can be so readily used to produce the lesser, external goods, the ever-tempting voices of "the world, the flesh, and the devil" can drive the use of these technologies and their related occupations to such an inordinate extent that reason can no longer be used to limit their use. Mankind proudly pats itself on the back rather than thanks God for His selfless generosity.

For example, the technology to build a computer chip is a gift of God, and the benefits from this technology have so altered our lives that it is close to impossible to envision life without it. There are many ways in which this technology has been used to provide the higher goods of bringing people closer to God, enriching their souls, and providing for their bodily needs. Yet we all know to what pervasive extent this technology has also been used to fill our world with lesser goods—with gadgets we really don't need, yet which we have grown as a culture to believe we do need and cannot live without—and that any efforts to produce, advance, and extend these technologies are justified. But does the good of smartphones for the affluent in first-world nations justify the inordinate use of third-world factory workers in sweatshops or near-slave laborers in rare-metal mines in Africa? These poor third-world workers are not producing anything that meets their own bodily needs, nor is their work in any way naturally limited: they will work as long as their employer demands—as many hours and days as he demands, to produce as many products as he deems necessary to produce the money he believes he needs—so they can scratch out enough money, they hope, to provide for the bodily needs of their families.

The problem is that we live in a culture that places its highest values on the production of and lust for the lesser material goods; even the "poor" have been redefined by our government, not for their lack of the higher goods to meet their bodily and spiritual needs but for their inability to procure the lesser material goods that our culture deems their rights in our civilized state. Far too many people on welfare, labeled "poor" by our government, have cell phones, HDTVs, cable, air conditioning, more than one car per family, and, per government reports, are not starving but generally overweight. (This last point is complicated, because too often the only food and drink available to the poor is less than beneficial, full of trans fats and sugar, etc., whereas healthy food, such as fresh produce, is either too expensive or, for those living in the inner city, often simply inaccessible.)

We live in a culture, a world, that has it all "bass-ackwards"—that rewards and honors those who dedicate their entire lives to producing, promoting, and getting rich on the lesser material goods of this world, all of which remain in the "box" when the lid is closed on this life. Yet this culture of ours also looks askance at, even denigrates, those who have chosen a simpler life, who have dedicated their lives to providing for their families those things—and maybe only those things—that are most essential. Just think how many in our culture—how we ourselves—too often look down on families who have little more than enough material goods to provide for their bodily needs, yet their existence is far more in line with that promoted and lived by our Lord Jesus, His disciples, Saint Francis of Assisi, and the myriad of other holy Christians throughout the ages.

The problem is that these twisted values of our culture have so infiltrated every aspect of our lives that an increasing number of those dedicated to providing the basic bodily needs of our world—food, clothing, shelter, and even spiritual enrichment—are encouraged to do so primarily to accumulate more and more money—not to provide the top three levels of goodness but to fill their lives with lesser material things. Agribusinessmen, as modern farmers prefer to be called, for example, now use hundreds of thousands of dollars of high-tech equipment to farm thousands of acres to provide high-yield hybrid and genetically modified crops. They do this to make sufficient profit to provide not only the food, drink, clothing, and shelter their families need but also the external goods they deem necessary to consider themselves as equally progressive as the city dwellers they see portrayed on network television as the models of "the American dream." (See appendix 2 for some suggestions on financial planning based on the teachings of Saint Thomas Aquinas as summarized by Bishop George Speltz.)

So, if any of this is true, what does it say to most of us who not only have chosen but believe God has called us to focus our time, talent, and energies on occupations other than "husbandry" and to live in non-rural settings? Regardless of where we live or what we must do to provide sustenance for ourselves and our families, here are a few suggestions of where we might begin:

- Pray for forgiveness for all the ways in which our lives have been driven by "want of wealth and what it can buy";

- Meditate daily on the New Testament teachings on gospel simplicity. Pray for clarity and guidance as to how the Lord wants us to live this out in our particular circumstances;

- Look more closely at our "stuff," and recognize how much of it consists of lesser, nonessential goods. Consider how much of our lives has become subsumed in accumulating and hoarding these nonessentials;

- Every time we believe we must go shopping, consider whether what we are tempted to buy is necessary for the bodily and spiritual needs of our family or just another unnecessary, lesser material entanglement that one day we may wish we had never bought in the first place; and

- Pray for the freeing grace of detachment. How many things do we own that if taken away would truly devastate us? Ask God to give us the grace to start letting go of things, even giving them away, to friends, family, and especially agencies that serve the needy.

Setting a sustainable Example

As I put these thoughts down on paper, I was confronted by the fact of how poorly I have followed my own advice in simplifying our lives and detaching ourselves from the endless accumulation of stuff. It's truly debilitating how the devil has made getting rid of stuff at least ten times harder than getting it, which is why it's so much better to adopt an attitude of simplicity and detachment as early as possible in one's life, and especially in a marriage.

Along with the bullet points I list earlier, I think we need to recognize that, even if we believe that our present accumulation of stuff is not harmful to our spiritual life, it may be setting an unsustainable example for our children and grandchildren. By grace, we may have grown sufficiently detached from our stuff; we may have convinced ourselves that if we lost it all tomorrow, we would be just fine; we may even have ceased buying more and more, becoming content with living more simply. The question then arises whether it is necessary to continue divesting ourselves of the remaining stuff that surrounds us. "I just might need that widget tomorrow, and if it's gone, I may regret it!" How much more loudly does our accumulation speak than the convictions of our heart? Does our remaining accumulation present a continuing contradiction to our well-meaning words? Our conflicting examples may be setting up our children and grandchildren for a life of even more escalating accumulation, because the cultural river in which our children swim tells them that success is measured by how much more stuff they attain than their parents.

Allow me to add a personal illustration. The elderly mother of a very close friend (names withheld to protect the innocent) died recently. She had always been a discerning collector of books, vinyl records, audio and video recordings, teddy bears, figurines, pottery, and dolls. Especially during the years after her husband died, and as she became less mobile, she increasingly surrounded herself with the stuff that brought her joy. Maybe it was because she had been born immediately after the 1929 stock-market crash and had lived through the poverty of the Depression and then WWII that she so encamped herself within the security of things.

It wasn't until after her passing, when her children began taking inventory of the estate, that they became fully aware of the extent to which she had evolved from a collector into an addicted hoarder. Closets, cupboards, shelves, display cabinets, and that off-the-beaten-path attic were overflowing with thousands of records, cassette tapes, VHS tapes, and CDs. At an average of $10 per item, the original cost must have topped $50,000! When purchased, these recordings may have held some investment value, but with the accelerating *progress* of today's digital age of instant accessibility and gratification, this physical cache of recordings has become essentially worthless. And the collections of bears, dolls, figurines, bottles, porcelain houses, and pottery, also originally worth thousands of dollars, are of little redeemable value, except to those who are serious collectors, or perhaps who themselves have evolved into addicted hoarders.

Now the family is stuck wondering what to do with all this stuff. It so happened that they themselves had already become somewhat convicted about living simpler lives, trying to detach themselves from our culture's constant pressure to buy and hoard more and more, but now they have inherited a second house, which because of nostalgia will be hard to sell, and which is overflowing with essentially worthless stuff that also will be difficult to sell. And because they have become convinced of the necessity of living more simply, they are hesitant to pass this stuff on to burden someone else's life, even by just giving it away. They could bag it all up and throw it away, but is this being a good steward of the dreams of their mother, who bought this stuff thinking it would be of some value to pass on to her children and grandchildren? She wanted to bless their lives; but she had no idea to what extent her collections had become a curse. The family continues to sit and muddle over all this, with coffee and scotch.

When we die, and our closets, shelves, cupboards, display cabinets, garages, and storage units (or barns) are opened for inventory, what will our "collecting" tell our children about our commitment to living Christ-centered, simpler lives?

Consider to what extent learning and achieving true contentment requires that we spend the remainder of our lives divesting ourselves of unnecessary things beyond our bodily and spiritual needs, to live more and more simply, whether we live in a rural setting or a high-rise apartment in downtown Manhattan. Doesn't this seem like the best thing we can do not just for ourselves but also for our children and grandchildren? Then, through the assistance of grace, we may be able to live out what our Lord and his disciples taught:

> Sell your possessions, and give alms; provide yourselves with purses that do not grow old, with a treasure in the heavens that does not fail, where no thief approaches and no moth destroys. (Lk 12:33)

Our Lord said pretty much the same in His *Sermon on the Mount*, to all who might listen:

> Do not lay up for yourselves treasures on earth, where moth and rust consume and where thieves break in and steal, but lay up for yourselves treasures in heaven, where neither moth nor rust consumes and where thieves do not break in and steal. *For where your treasure is, there will your heart be also.* (Mt 6:19–21)

Practice Personal Subsidiarity

I believe an amazing, even mystical, sense of contentment comes from practicing personal subsidiarity. In his introduction to *Flee to the Fields*, Dr. Tobias Lanz gave the following helpful definition of social subsidiarity:

> Social subsidiarity ... holds that an individual should rely on the most basic levels of social and technical complexity to achieve his goals. Higher levels are called upon only when the lower echelon is insufficient to the task. Thus, by relying on the household, family, community, and nature's bounty to provide

> as many basic needs as possible, people could free themselves from economic dependence and the political control of the plutocrats, and thereby regain a modicum of human dignity and freedom.[22]

Applying this in personal practice, we can examine how we spend our money, where we place our investments, where we shop, and from where we purchase our goods, beginning first close to home and only then working outward. Over my many years, I've found it amazing how drastically contentment is inversely proportional to the expanding availability of shopping options. And this has become infinitely true with the advent of the Internet. Having no limits to products can make contentment, at least for some of us, unattainable.

An Even Bolder Suggestion

Up until now, I've suggested some steps toward learning and choosing contentment; these include (1) beginning right where we are, (2) loving the people God has put right now into our lives, (3) focusing on the stable and established in the world around us, (4) recognizing the presence of God and His love in creation, (5) reducing the incessant voices that try to control our lives, and (6) living more simply. All these steps are in line with the teachings of our Lord and His Church, and, admittedly, each requires willful sacrifice, empowered by grace.

This next suggestion, I realize, however, is only for "those to whom this has been given." This is what Jesus said about those of His followers called to the celibate life (see Mt 19:11–12). The same is true, though, for those called to live a more self-sufficient life on the land. I hesitate to include this in the list because, indeed, not all are called to this, maybe only a few. There was a time, though, just as recently as the childhood of our grandparents, when the majority of people in this world were more self-sufficient or at least trying to be. They admittedly led a simpler life and likely chose contentment with few thoughts or interests in upward mobility.

At this point, some readers might be wondering whether I consider myself one of those "to whom this has been given." Well, for the past twenty-five years, my family and I have focused a large portion of our time, talents, and resources towards growing more self-sufficient on our rural "cottage farm," and I can't deny that, even in the time it has taken to write and rewrite this book, I have struggled over this question. And maybe by the time this book has landed in your hands, I will have been led even to a different conclusion.

What I have come to realize, however, is how much this is more a corporate than an individual decision. If you are an individual hermit, with few, if any, attachments, you are, therefore, free to discern for yourself and initiate all the radical changes necessary to live a self-sufficient life off the grid, raising chickens, hand-milking a Jersey, pasturing cattle, sheep, or pigs for meat, and fighting weeds in a garden, planted "inch by inch and row by row."[23] But, just as in the advice given by Christ in Matthew 19, if you are married and have children and grandchildren, the permutations of attachments and responsibilities make these kind of countercultural changes exponentially more difficult—and specifically the means of discerning God's call to this vocation.

As for Marilyn and me, we have progressed an amazing distance down the road of self-sufficiency, but extended family and business responsibilities, as well as my own waffling convictions and aging frame, leave the trajectory of our self-sufficiency in the hands of God.

As I consider what my wife, Marilyn, and I need to do now, out here as empty-nesters on our "cottage farm" in the years ahead, there are some things I have come to learn. Just because we left the city to live out here on this rural property, or because we established this "cottage farm" for our boys and brought them up on this land, learning right beside me how to "farm," that does not, therefore, automatically mean that God has called my boys—or even me—to be farmers. There are myriads of publications and blogs exhorting people to hightail it out of the city and return to the farm, to save our country by re-establishing traditional American small-farm culture, and to avoid the coming Tribulation by becoming self-sufficient and off-the-grid. And I can't deny that there were times I at least tried to preach and live this separatist agrarian gospel; nor can I deny that I believe there is great value and hope in becoming more self-sufficient and less attached to this frenetic world around us.

But now I see that we must not douse ourselves and especially our children with false guilt over their supposed responsibility to take over this farm—or, might I add, any family business. We may have done all this for them, which is truly generous, charitable, and humble, but we need to remember that they need to be free to discern what God is calling them to do.

It may have been God's desire for us to live and bring up our sons on this farm, in a rural enclave where they could receive the blessings of a more traditional, rural education and culture—less tainted by the crazy wokeness and apostasy of the surrounding culture—but not necessarily so they themselves would remain in this rural safe stronghold. Rather, it may have been so that they would be better prepared to go forth to live and preach the gospel in the midst of this fallen world.

I see that this has happened with our three sons. Actually, in spite of my many, many shortcomings, and my wife's and my less-than-perfect attempts at parenting, all three of our sons are not only still active in the Church, but (at least) say they loved growing up out here on our rural "cottage farm." It has become increasingly obvious, however, that continuing on the farm, let alone taking it over after I've "retired," is not where their hearts are leading them.

Especially within the agrarian community, there is a persistent accusatory finger pointed back at the thousands of children who have left farming for life elsewhere, blaming them for the demise of family farms in America. This is unfair as well as ignorantly uncharitable. There was a time when families had no choice but to farm, to put food on their tables as well as have some means of making a living. Yes, it was a good and wholesome life for many; but the reason so many left was that it was not necessarily so for everyone.

Today, for most, living on a rural farm is a privilege and needs to be understood as a calling, not an obligation. Otherwise, one cannot be free to hear the whispering voice of God, whether through the pines and leaves, the crops and animals, the creeks and stars of a rural environment, or the still, small voice that still beckons even along the perilous streets of a crowded city.

I've grown to see that God called my family out to this rural property not necessarily to become farmers but to discover, together with our sons, what the gospel of Jesus Christ is really all about. It's certainly about faith, the sacraments, the Church, and all of that, of course. But it's mostly about learning and choosing contentment, through love and humility; hard work, forgiveness, and humility; detachment, simplicity, sacrifice, and humility; courage and others-centeredness; oh, and did I mention, humility?

As a summary to this chapter, let's consider what some of the saints and recognized spiritual writers have said about the importance of living simply:

> There are two wings that raise a man above earthly things—simplicity and purity. Simplicity must inspire his purpose, and purity his affection. Simplicity reaches out after God; purity discovers and enjoys Him.
>
> Thomas à Kempis, *The Imitation of Christ*

> It is when I possess least that I have the fewest worries, and the Lord knows that, as far as I can tell, I am more afflicted when there is excess of anything than when there is lack of it.
>
> Saint Teresa of Avila, *The Way of Perfection*

> Property, wealth, diversions, amusements are often obstacles to the attainment of truth, beauty, celebration, delight, and love. They are not evil in themselves, of course, but the fact is that they allure us to fasten on them for themselves. They become finite crutches that distract and lead us away from our genuine quenching. Pulled to them, we cannot be pulled to God.
>
> Thomas Dubay, *Happy Are You Poor*

Among those who make profession of following the maxims of Christ, simplicity ought to be held in great esteem; for, among the wise of this world there is nothing more contemptible or despicable than this. Yet it is a virtue most worthy of love, because it leads us straight to the kingdom of God, and, at the same time, wins for us the affection of men.

St. Vincent de Paul

7

REDUCE FINANCIAL ENTANGLEMENTS

I would strongly suggest that trying to live a simpler life also means making what some might consider radical changes in our financial entanglements. Nothing undercuts any chance for contentment and, instead, binds us as individuals, as families, and as a nation to the accelerating grip of our changing economic culture than our debts and our investments. The more we can get out of debt and, as the good Distributists have been telling us for years, situated securely on our own piece of land with our own home, no matter how small and meager, the more we can become detached from the effects of any craziness that might occur in our nation or world. Even if all the markets rebound, and our friends wag their fingers that we were foolish not to have placed all our eggs in the basket of progress, they actually have only moved one minute step towards an unreachable goal of increasing maladjustment and instability.

When I first began, ten years ago, writing the articles that would eventually evolve into this book, the stock market had just reached an all-time high—a month later, it had dropped 1,000 points, vacillating 300 points up and down every day. Ever since, even though the Dow has several times broken all-time records, still, the stock market has only become increasingly unpredictable.

The true problem arises from what was assumed, for example, by all the candidates in all the parties in all the presidential elections of the last few decades: that every American should have the opportunity to attain the American dream; every American should be able to become a member of the "middle class" (in this supposedly "classless" culture). However, the more we—as individuals, families, and a culture—define the "American dream" as the accumulation of more and more things (which requires increasingly more and more money), the more we set our families and culture on an unsustainable death spiral towards political and economic chaos.

On this trajectory, the poverty level continually gets redefined upwards, and the expectations and "rights" increase proportionately. As a result, government subsidies and entitlement programs must increase—as of this writing, nearly half of the American population is living on government assistance. Add to this the more than one million undocumented illegal aliens who have crossed our borders in the past decade, who are mostly being supported by our tax dollars. On this trajectory and under these assumptions, abortion, contraception, and euthanasia, along with mood-altering drugs, and even the endorsement of relationships that cannot produce children have become the necessary tools of those in power to control the population so that more of those who remain can rise to the material level of the "middle class." In this quest, our government has amassed a 36.1-trillion-dollar debt, increasing at an exponential rate, all to satisfy a material-hungry populace. Who will pay for this? Not us, for, like Pontius Pilate, the present generation washes its hands of all guilt, leaving the payment to our children and grandchildren. (Does anyone really have a workable solution to our national debt? As I write this, the *US Debt Clock* estimates that each citizen's share of our national debt is $107,381!)[24]

The only solution is for all in America, from the top down, to learn to be contented with far less; not just for the "haves" to share their wealth with the "have-nots" but for the entire "American dream" to be redefined on a more realistic, sustainable scale. I have little hope that this will happen in America, or in any of today's first-world nations, for the last half of the last century was all about raising the expectations of everyone's right to financial progress and independence. Once this toothpaste is out of the tube, it's impossible to put it back, short of resetting expectations through a major worldwide crisis, such as a depression or war, or through pervasive conversions of heart. There is little we can do to stop any of this, unless we, as individuals and families, consider making, as I said at the beginning of this section, "radical changes in [our] financial entanglements."

Even one of the most influential players in our modern, industrial, progressivist culture, Bill Gates, admitted ten years ago that accelerating technologies, many of which he had a hand in developing, will drastically change the work environment even more for our children and grandchildren. Speaking at the American Enterprise Institute in Washington, D.C., he said:

> Software substitution, whether it's for drivers or waiters or nurses … [is] progressing. … Technology over time will reduce demand for jobs, particularly at the lower end of skill set. … *Twenty years from now, labor demand for lots of skill sets will be substantially lower.* I don't think people have that in their mental model."[25]

The more we can free ourselves from the clutching, paralyzing control of debt, adopting what we will discuss later as our Lord's call to a "poverty of spirit," the freer we will be to choose what is necessary to learn and grow in true contentment.

Consider this. About ten years ago, the Catholic Church held an Extraordinary Synod in Rome on the Family. As never before in history, the world could now follow nearly every word, debate by debate, of every committee of bishops, and the commentaries flowed and frothed freely. Progressives of every stripe hoped the Church would change its centuries-old unaltered views on marriage, divorce, remarriage, homosexuality, and gay marriage, and conservatives feared that cultural momentum would carry the day. In the midst of this worldwide coverage, a Catholic group promoting lifestyles contrary to Church teaching and Christian tradition announced that it had initiated a lobbying effort to influence eight of the most conservative bishops in America. There is much that I found troubling about the convictions and lobbying efforts of this group, but the most enigmatic information that emerged was that the corporate partners of this group were "large corporations like American Airlines, Apple, Google, Microsoft, Bank of America, Northrop Grumman, Chevron, Lexus, Goldman Sachs, Coca-Cola and PepsiCo."[26]

When I read this article I was flying on American Airlines; I was reading it on an Apple computer; I had used Google to find the article; at least half of the software on my computer is by Microsoft; some of the investments that paid for my trip are in Bank of America; the plane in which I was flying likely had parts manufactured by Northrop Grumman; I bought gas for my pickup at the Chevron station near the airport; I've lusted over buying a Lexus; the fingers of Goldman Sachs are everywhere; and throughout my trip I've quaffed many a Diet Coke, or Diet Pepsi if Diet Coke wasn't available. All I do is provide funds for this lobbyist group committed to undercutting the longstanding teachings of the Church on family and sexual morality.

How do we extricate ourselves from this financial spiderweb? Is it even possible anymore? If it is the devil's goal to convince the world to become tolerant of every conceivable lifestyle, this will require the attacks of many lobbying groups from many fronts. Besides the whispering that every person hears in their inner mind, lobbying groups like the one mentioned need lots and lots of money. How better than to champion technologies to which the world has become so addicted that they can no longer imagine living without? And thousands of people lined up all night long to be the first to own the new iPhone 16, when there really was nothing essentially wrong with the iPhone 15, 14, 13, 12, et cetera, or any of the previous models, or even the most basic flip phones. Have the technologies enticed, captured, and carried us all away?

Today, nearly every dollar we spend goes to companies, particularly technology companies, that use our money to promote lifestyles we personally may consider immoral or are contrary to the values of our faith. To what extent are we culpable for this funding, particularly if we have come to know about a corporation's spending practices?

I can hear in my mind the voices even of friends who belittle my concerns. They merely respond, "It has always been this way—even the first-century Christians had to pay tax to Rome! And besides, it would be impossible to extricate ourselves—we'd have to quit buying anything!"

But has it always been what it is today? Here's an experiment that probably anyone my age can do. When I was four, in the mid-fifties, my parents had low-level management jobs with the local telephone company. My father had worked his way up from an installer into management, and my mother had risen from an operator to an engineer—both without college. My father had just completed building our home, from a kit, on a half-acre lot in our small northwestern suburban Ohio town.

With a little bit of reflection, I think I've come up with a pretty good guess at what their expenses were:

- Mortgage with local bank;
- Ford car loan with local bank;
- Gas and maintenance through local gas station;
- Electric, gas, waste, phone, and water bills through local companies;
- A television set, that received 5 free local stations;
- A radio set that received about 10 free local stations;
- The local newspaper by subscription;
- I don't think they had health insurance; we only went to the doctor's office for crisis care; otherwise, the doctor made house calls;
- Both had retirement plans provided by their employer;
- And they paid federal, Ohio, and local taxes, as well as Social Security and Medicare.

Now, I am quite certain that back in the fifties none of the national or local companies to which my parents were paying money were funneling funds to promote lifestyles contrary to their beliefs: these corporations were not yet funding action groups promoting abortion, contraception, euthanasia, guns for terrorists, or same-sex marriage. And none of these companies were being run by people who were openly promoting or practicing any of these issues. Certainly, some of these corporate leaders may have been philanderers, adulterers, or thieves—but they were not openly advocating these lifestyles, and if/when they were caught, they were generally ostracized, fired, and sometimes prosecuted. I doubt that it ever crossed my parents' minds that any of these companies would be contributing to organizations promoting alternative lifestyles. They would have been shocked to discover this—as they became appalled as these lifestyles became more and more accepted, and then promoted, in our culture.

Today, nearly every one of these companies is somehow invested in promoting alternative lifestyles and values, either directly or indirectly, and often blatantly so. And particularly, these corporations are providing the very technological entertainment and networking services to which we as a culture have become dependent, dare I say addicted.

What is most striking to me about this is that this has all happened within my lifetime. What will our culture be like for our children and grandchildren? We are so drowning in this soup that it seems beyond our capabilities to divest ourselves from any of this. And the devil laughs.

All I can say is that, after many years of stressing over the weight of debt, due mostly to poor financial decisions, I'm immeasurably grateful, to the generous mercy of God, that my wife and I were able to enter these "twilight years" debt free.

8

Practice Poverty of Spirit

Living more simply begins and ends with detachment, which our Lord most clearly described in the new gospel that He gave to those who desired to grow closer to Him and thereby enter the kingdom. (I've written of this in much more detail elsewhere.)[27] Jesus gave this in a sermon on a mount of grass, out in a field, to people gathered around Him, enjoying the wind and the sun, the songs of birds and the camaraderie of family and friends.

He talked about being blessed, about the qualities that this requires, and about rewards. We've all heard these Beatitudes, and often they're interpreted as separate promises referring, possibly, to separate groups of individuals:

> Blessed are the poor in spirit, for theirs is the kingdom of heaven.
>
> Blessed are those who mourn, for they shall be comforted.
>
> Blessed are the meek, for they shall inherit the earth.
>
> Blessed are those who hunger and thirst for righteousness, for they shall be satisfied.
>
> Blessed are the merciful, for they shall obtain mercy.
>
> Blessed are the pure in heart, for they shall see God.
>
> Blessed are the peacemakers, for they shall be called sons of God.
>
> Blessed are those who are persecuted for righteousness' sake, for theirs is the kingdom of heaven.

> Blessed are you when men revile you and persecute you and utter all kinds of evil against you falsely on my account. Rejoice and be glad, for your reward is great in heaven, for so men persecuted the prophets who were before you. (Mt 5:3–12)

Years ago in my readings, I discovered, through the writings of several Church Fathers—Saints Chromatius of Aquileia (AD 340–408), Gregory of Nyssa (AD 335–386), and Pope Leo the Great (d. 461)—how the Beatitudes were understood as a staircase of growing closer to Christ. Pope Leo wrote: "Thus whoever longs to attain eternal blessedness can now recognize the steps that lead to that high happiness."[28]

"High happiness" and "eternal blessedness" are essentially other ways of saying true and eternal contentment. In other words, Jesus was not merely saying that God blesses those who find themselves impotently in a state of poverty, mourning, meekness, et cetera, but rather, He was commanding His hearers to willfully *choose* poverty of spirit, mourning, meekness, et cetera. From the perspective of Saints Chromatius, Gregory of Nyssa, and Leo the Great, Jesus was telling His followers that each Beatitude was a step or "rung" that leads to a next Beatitude, and therefore becomes a foundation for the next.

The Fathers explained the first three Beatitudes as steps in which we choose detachment from the false gods that prevent us from attaining contentment: detachment from the things of this world (***poverty of spirit***), from sin (***those who mourn*** for their sins), and from ourselves (***the meek***). These first three detachments were modeled by our Lord's first disciples when they "immediately left their nets and followed him" (Mk 1:18). All of Jesus' instructions on discipleship begin here, and one must not turn back: "No one who puts his hand to the plow and looks back is fit for the kingdom of God" (Lk 9:62). This was why Saint Paul warned the newly baptized pagan converts in Ephesus not to fall back into their former sinful lifestyles but exhorted them:

> Put off the old man, which belongs to your former manner of life and is corrupt through deceitful lusts, and be renewed in the spirit of your minds, and put on the new man, created after the likeness of God in true righteousness and holiness. (Eph 4:22–24)

Saint Leo the Great, in his sermons on the Beatitudes, made an imporant clarification:

> But when [our Lord] says *Blessed are the poor in spirit*, he shows that the kingdom of heaven is to be given to those who are distinguished by their humility of soul rather than by their lack of worldly goods.[29]

In other words, the steps of the Beatitudes begin not so much with detachment from worldly goods, i.e., to become like the poor, but rather to seek humility of soul. All three first steps are about growing in humility, by detaching from the world, sin, and self, and this humility of soul shifts the focus of our mind and heart away from the foundations of false contentment towards the source of true contentment: to "***hunger and thirst for righteousness***."

I love our Lord's use of the emotive words "hunger and thirst" because his audience, to a man, understood these necessary desires, which can only be satisfied by our choosing and acting to fill this void, which in this case is "righteousness." True lasting contentment can only come from first breaking the false foundations of attachment to this world, to sin, and to ourselves, and rebuilding a "firm foundation" of righteousness.

I would suggest that too often this is where most expressions of the gospel today end: clean out the false attachments in your life so you can fill up your life with good attachments and consequently attain happiness! The television, radio, and Internet overflow with evangelists preaching this, which essentially is a circular, self-focused gospel, all about doing all one can to make oneself happy, or content.

But this is not where Jesus ends. He goes on to step five: "***Blessed are the merciful***," which involves willingly obeying and living out righteousness: loving as Christ has loved us. If by grace we do this, our Lord says that it is through this that we, in turn, will receive and experience the reward of God's mercy. There's a direct connect here. When Jesus taught His disciples how to pray the "Our Father", He made this important qualification:

> For if you forgive men their trespasses, your heavenly Father also will forgive you; but if you do not forgive men their trespasses, neither will your Father forgive your trespasses. (Mt 6:14–15)

Seeking contentment directly as a self-focused goal is counterproductive; it's in forgiving others that we are forgiven; it's in being merciful to others that we receive mercy; and it's in helping others learn and grow in contentment that we ourselves can find true contentment.

Our Lord suggests this very thing, for the next step after our being merciful is where He speaks of "***the pure in heart***," the reward of which is the gift of "***seeing God***." A person with a pure heart is one whose inner life has been cleansed of the distractions of the world, the flesh, and the devil and by grace has turned outward in mercy to others.

I'll pick up later with the remaining Beatitudes, but it's crucial to understand that we can still fall back, once we realize that these steps have not led to deep feelings of contentment; rather, we have merely reached the stage of discovering our lifelong mission, the "obedience of faith" in which we are called to live by grace every day until God calls us home.

We can become complacent in our presumptions, assuming that, through our efforts in obedience to Christ, we have arrived, and as a result blindly fall backwards, glorying in our successes, even arrogantly wallowing in the external symbols of our spiritual progress.

Admittedly, these steps as presented are intimidating; each alone can seem out of reach, let alone a step to the next. Just making any headway toward detaching ourselves from the world seems impossible, in this age when our very existence seems dependent upon technologies, politics, and economic entanglements that the first-century Christians could never have imagined. The impossibility of these steps, in fact, is why so many of Jesus' hearers refused to follow Him. Yet Jesus did not back down from the importance of these challenges, for later in the same sermon, He said: "You, therefore, must be perfect, as your heavenly Father is perfect" (Mt 5:48). He also said, though, that this radical living was to be augmented with prayer, fasting, and almsgiving (Mt 6:1–18) and that if we asked, sought, and knocked, He would help us (Mt 7:7–12).

Just realizing the significance and promise of these Beatitudes is a start—it's the self-affirming evidence that God's grace is at work. Any effort we make to at least begin detaching ourselves from the world, sin, and self, initiates a hunger and thirst in our hearts for righteousness, empowering us to do what is most important: to be merciful to others as God has been merciful to us, which gives us a glimmer of the presence of God, which by grace can give us the courage to begin stepping out in His Name.

The Two Ways

But what does poverty of spirit, or detachment from the world, really mean, and how does one do it, especially in the context of our technological, digital, materialistic, and hedonistic twenty-first century? Please allow me to attempt this as simply and cleanly as possible (frankly, any deeper and I'm beyond my pay grade).

With all the definitions of detachment we may have heard (or not heard) throughout our lifetime, I would propose that true detachment involves living out what has long been called the ***Two Ways*** through the discipline of our senses, culminating in conversion of heart. Allow me to explain.

The simplest way to understand all of Scripture, all of salvation history, and all of our lives from birth to death and judgment, is through the hermeneutic of the *Two Ways.* If one has "eyes to see and ears to hear," one can detect it running throughout

Scripture, behind every psalm or proverb, covenant, law, statute, or commandment; it's woven in and through Christ's *Sermon on the Mount* and all of His teachings; it's there in every New Testament epistle; and it's essentially there from beginning to end in the *Catechism of the Catholic Church.*

Basically, our loving, merciful Creator God, from the beginning, has said to His created sons and daughters—and put within the conscience of every person who's ever lived—that there are *Two Ways* we can follow, most often called the Righteous Way and the Wicked Way. We can turn, by grace through faith, to follow His way, trusting, fearing, loving, and serving Him, as His adopted children, or we can turn away, rejecting grace, to follow our own way, or maybe someone else's way other than that of our Creator God. To put it crudely, as a frustrated dad might say to a rebellious son, "It's either my way or the highway."

One of the earliest Christian writings outside of the New Testament, called the *Didache*, described these *Two Ways* in detail. The author called them the *Way of Life* and the *Way of Death*, giving a detailed list of the do's and don'ts of each *Way*.

The most interesting thing one discovers, however, through careful reflection on Scripture, is that the primary means by which one follows either the *Righteous* or the *Wicked Way* is through what a person does with his bodily senses: with his eyes, ears, lips, hands, knees, feet, his whole body, leading to what fills his mind and heart.

For example, here's just a taste of the hundreds of Scriptures suggesting this:

> [F]or the Lord knows the ***way of the righteous***, but the ***way of the wicked*** will perish. (Ps 1:6)

> But my ***eyes*** are toward thee, O Lord God; in thee I seek refuge; leave me not defenseless! (Ps 141:8)

> He who ***walks*** righteously and ***speaks*** uprightly, who despises the gain of oppressions, who shakes his ***hands***, lest they hold a bribe, who stops his ***ears*** from ***hearing*** of bloodshed and shuts his ***eyes*** from ***looking*** upon evil. (Isa 33:15)

> I said, "I will guard my ***ways***, that I may not sin with my ***tongue***; I will bridle my ***mouth***, so long as the wicked are in my presence." (Ps 39:1)
>
> Take heed to the ***path*** of your ***feet***, then all your ***ways*** will be sure. (Prov 4:26)
>
> And the ***tongue*** is a fire. The ***tongue*** is an unrighteous world among our members, staining the whole ***body***, setting on fire the cycle of nature, and set on fire by hell. (James 3:6)
>
> I the LORD search the ***mind*** and try the ***heart***, to give to every man according to his ***ways***, according to the fruit of his doings. (Jer 17:10)

Why did our Lord use such strong hyperbole when he warned that it would be better to have one's right hand cut off or right eye plucked out than to sin with either of these? Because it is through what a person does with his eyes, ears, lips, hands, knees, feet, mind, body, and ultimately his heart, that determines whether by grace that person has chosen to turn, follow, and attach himself to God's *Righteous Way* or to have turned away—turning his back on God.

The unanimous witness of Scripture, Old and New, is that when we turn away from God, rejecting His *Righteous Way* for the *Wicked Way*, we bring upon ourselves His wrath. We hear this from Saint Paul in his letter to the Christians in Rome:

> But by your hard and impenitent heart you are storing up wrath for yourself on the day of wrath when God's righteous judgment will be revealed. For he will render to every man according to his works: to those who by patience in well-doing seek for glory and honor and immortality, he will give eternal life; but for those who are factious and do not obey the truth, but obey wickedness, there will be wrath and fury. (Rom 2:5–8)

There are many ways to understand this, but essentially this happens because when by grace we turn and walk in His *Righteous*

Way, we move closer to Him, we walk with Him, beside Him, and in the process, we come to *know* Him more intimately, and He comes to *know us*. But when we turn away and walk away from Him, putting distance between Him and us, we grow to know Him less, and He us. When we walk with Him, He can help us; when we turn away, He can't. We see this most clearly illustrated in our Lord's parable of the Prodigal Son.

Toward the end of the *Sermon on the Mount*, there's a troubling passage that many readers just skip over and ignore. But Jesus warned:

> Not every one who says to me, "Lord, Lord," shall enter the kingdom of heaven, but he who does the will of my Father who is in heaven. On that day many will say to me, "Lord, Lord, did we not prophesy in your name, and cast out demons in your name, and do many mighty works in your name?" And then will I declare to them, "***I never knew you***; depart from me, you evildoers." (Mt 7:21–23)

"I never knew you." A person can appear to be walking the *Righteous Way* through his good deeds, his endless seemingly selfless acts, even through his diligent practice of the rituals and disciplines of his particular religious tradition, but if otherwise, his eyes, ears, mouth, hands, knees, feet, whole being, mind, and heart are not really on the path towards God, then there is no real relationship; they're not walking together, and they never really come to know each other. Lord, help us.

Detachment

So, what is *detachment,* but turning our eyes, ears, lips, hands, knees, feet, our whole being, our mind and heart, away from things that are not of God, turning all that we are back into God's direction, and by grace attaching ourselves to Him: seeing the things He wants us to focus our eyes upon; listening to what He wants us to hear; bending our knees before Him and not before one of the myriad of false gods in our present world; and the same with all of our senses, so that in time our bodies become what Saint Paul challenged the Roman Christians:

> I appeal to you therefore, brethren, by the mercies of God, ***to present your bodies as a living sacrifice, holy and acceptable to God***, which is your spiritual worship. (Rom 12:1)

Saint Paul goes on to describe this detachment from the *Wicked Way* and turning to the *Righteous Way* when he says:

> Do not be conformed to this world but be transformed by the renewal of your mind, that you may prove what is the will of God, what is good and acceptable and perfect. (Rom. 12:2)

What today are your eyes attached to? What do you mostly see, day in, day out? Or listen to? Or what are you doing with your hands? There are things we use our hands for that the writers of Scripture and the early Church Fathers never imagined: remote controls, keyboards, mice, et cetera. And what are we doing with our feet? Where do they take us? And again, our feet are being carried along in ways our ancestors never imagined—on bicycles, cars, trains, airplanes, skateboards, Segways, et cetera. Where do we choose to go with the time God has given us?

Detachment requires us to consider these things. To some extent, it's not as crucial whether we live in the largest mansion in America or in a "van down by the river," because a poor man's senses and heart can be obsessed with gaining wealth for himself, while a rich man's senses and heart can be focused on using his wealth for the needs of the world.

What's most important is to what or to whom our senses, our whole being, and consequently our hearts, are attached. This is why Jesus warned in His *Sermon* that we cannot serve two masters, God and mammon: we can't walk along two contradictory paths. It's either His Way or none at all.

I hesitate even more to make the following references, for it will surely label me a doomsayer, but, given the present state of our national and world economies as well as our perilous political tension, the fifth chapter of the prophet Jeremiah is worth reading prayerfully. His original target was rebellious Israel, but since the Word of God is a living message with many layers of meaning and application, we benefit by recognizing the relevance of his warnings to our modern world:

> Run to and fro through the streets of Jerusalem, look and take note! Search her squares to see if you can find a man, one who does justice and seeks truth; that I may pardon her. Though they say, "As the LORD lives," yet they swear falsely.
>
> O LORD, do not thy eyes look for truth? Thou hast smitten them, but they felt no anguish; thou hast consumed them, but they refused to take correction They have made their faces harder than rock; they have refused to repent.
>
> Then I said, "These are only the poor, they have no sense; for they do not know the ***way of the LORD***, the law of their God. I will go to the great, and will speak to them; For they know the ***way of the LORD***, the law of their God."
>
> But they all alike had broken the yoke, they had burst the bonds. (Jer 5:1–5)

Then comes the rhetorical conclusion of the Lord:

> "Shall I not punish them for these things?" says the Lord; "And shall I not avenge myself on a nation such as this?" (Jer 5:9)

And His answer:

> "Behold, I am bringing upon you a nation from afar, O house of Israel," says the LORD. "It is an enduring nation, it is an ancient nation, *a nation whose language you do not know, nor can you understand what they say*." (Jer 5:15)

For Israel, it was Babylon, but for America—for Western civilization—might it be Russia, China, North Korea, radical Islamic terrorists, or the drug cartels of northern Mexico?

Regardless of whether these ancient prophecies have anything to do with our present age, still the message remains: Our Lord continues to call us to detachment and simplicity. This, however, must not be "attached" to a day or an hour, or to some potential financial or political crisis; rather, the truth that any one of us could be facing our Maker this night should be "warning" enough to awaken us to the dire need to simplify and detach our lives.

Living Each Day in Readiness

Everything expressed in this book has been about learning and choosing contentment basically through the normal hurdles of life. How we handle these, in Christ, will be the criteria that will determine our passage from this life to the next:

> For we must all appear before the judgment seat of Christ, so that each one may receive good or evil, according to what he has done in the body. (2 Cor 5:10)

And since we never know when this event might occur, we are called to be ready daily, and "watch, therefore, for you do not know on what day your Lord is coming" (Mt 24:42). It could be before you finish reading this page.

From the earliest days of the Church, Christian preachers and writers have exhorted us to live each day as if it's our last. We have no natural, divine right to a long life; what we've experienced has been a gift, and we should be grateful for every day, even through sorrow, sadness, failure, and frustration. As Saint Paul wrote:

> Besides this you know what hour it is, how ***it is full time now for you to wake from sleep***. For ***salvation is nearer to us now than when we first believed***; the night is far gone, the day is at hand. Let us then cast off the works of darkness and put on the armor of light; let us conduct ourselves becomingly as in the day, not in reveling and drunkenness, not in debauchery and licentiousness, not in quarreling and jealousy. (Rom 13:11–13)

Generally, I would assume that most of us (though we might assume we are always close to Jesus, especially through the sacraments) live our lives as if our final, critical meeting with our Lord is many years in the future—actually, many of us seem to live as if this future encounter is never going to happen. But we must not let these words of Scripture pass by without pausing and thinking, "Wait—he's talking to me! *Right now*, not someday way in the future. How should my life, starting *now*, by grace, be different, before it's too late?"

Long ago, Thomas à Kempis said it in a way probably more challenging than most moderns want to hear:

> You should order your every deed and thought as though today were the day of your death. Had you a good conscience, death would hold no terrors for you; even so, it were better to avoid sin than to escape death. If you are not ready to die today, will tomorrow find you better prepared?
>
> Blessed is the man who keeps the hour of his death always in mind, and daily prepares himself to die. Each morning remember that you may but live until evening; and in the evening, do not presume to promise yourself another day. Be ready at all times, and so live that death may never find you unprepared.
>
> Happy and wise is he who endeavours to be during his life as he wishes to be found at his death. For these things will afford us sure hope of a happy death: perfect contempt of the world; fervent desire to grow in holiness; love of discipline; the practice of penance; ready obedience; self-denial; the bearing of every trial for the love of Christ.[30]

The truth is, though, that most of us will live longer than that. Most of us will live for months, even years, on into an increasingly unpredictable future. How are we to prepare for this, for living every day as if it's our last, for possibly ten, twenty, or more years—and not just for ourselves, but for and with our spouse and family?

Again, as expressed several times before, I believe it helps to remember that, as human beings created in the image of God, we are both body and spirit—not mere biological beings, as the scientific materialistic atheists would tell us, destined to become nothing but fertilizer when we die, an insignificant part "in nature's chain," replenishing "Mother Earth" with what we irresponsibly took from her. Nor are we just heavenly spirits trapped in earthly bodies, such that only the destiny of our souls matter. Rather, we are both, which is why our faith has always emphasized the resurrection of the body: at death, our souls face a first, personal judgment; meanwhile, our earthly bodies remain in the ground, decaying, maybe for centuries, until our souls and spiritual bodies are reunited in the general resurrection on Judgment Day.

Living each day as if it will be our last means keeping our souls in grace, clean of sin, and free from the attachments to this world that we gain through the senses of our bodies. But since, according to God's providence, we may be gifted with decades of living, we must be good stewards of these bodies, so that our whole being, body and soul, can flourish in faith, hope, and love. As discussed earlier, for this to happen, we must provide the bodily goods we need (food, liquids, clothing, shelter) so that our entire person can thrive. At the same time, we must strive to become less attached to unnecessary external goods because, like the weeds and uninvited critters that take over our gardens each year, attachments can conspire to overpower, subdue, and conquer us, body and soul.

However, the biggest factor in determining what specific actions we need to take—daily or for years to come—is to recognize that salvation is not an individualistic quest. We are called to be faithful individuals within the Body of Christ, the Church. Our call to love our neighbor as Christ loves us means we are called, therefore, not only to be ready ourselves but to do all we can to help our neighbors live today as if it were their last day—to be ready spiritually to meet God: Are they living in grace? Are their souls pure? But this means recognizing that we and our neighbors—we and our families—may be living together for a long time! How can we help each other, while not becoming burdens to each other?

Certainly, we're called to help and care for each other, yet we can't presume on this—we can't merely assume that if we get sick or disabled, our children will pick up the slack. A glutton or a hoarder robs from the bodily needs of others, eventually becoming a burden on them through neglected health and accumulated attachments, and when he or she dies, such a person leaves behind an irresponsible burden of unnecessary goods. This means each of us ought to live healthy, simple, selfless lives, so that if one day we have no choice but to be a "burden," we will be as little of a burden as possible—maybe even a blessing.

Make More Time for Others

Most of this book so far has focused on how we ourselves can learn and choose true contentment, and not the false, shallow, fragile, and feelings-based contentment offered by the world around us. So, maybe it's time in our discussion to re-emphasize the second most important factor in learning and growing in contentment, which I touched on in chapter two: it's not about us; its about the others in our life.

I would suggest it's time to reflect on one of our Lord's most well known and too often misunderstood, if not ignored, parables of the kingdom (as well as of the *Two Ways*):

> When the Son of man comes in his glory, and all the angels with him, then he will sit on his glorious throne. Before him will be gathered all the nations, and he will separate them one from another as a shepherd separates the sheep from the goats, and he will place the sheep at his right hand, but the goats at the left.
>
> Then the King will say to those at his right hand, "Come, O blessed of my Father, inherit the kingdom prepared for you from the foundation of the world; for I was hungry and you gave me food, I was thirsty and you gave me drink, I was a stranger and you welcomed me, I was naked and you clothed me, I was sick and you visited me, I was in prison and you came to me."
>
> Then the righteous will answer him, "Lord, when did we see thee hungry and feed thee, or thirsty and give thee drink?

> And when did we see thee a stranger and welcome thee, or naked and clothe thee? And when did we see thee sick or in prison and visit thee?"
>
> And the King will answer them, "Truly, I say to you, as you did it to one of the least of these my brethren, you did it to me."
>
> Then he will say to those at his left hand, "Depart from me, you cursed, into the eternal fire prepared for the devil and his angels; for I was hungry and you gave me no food, I was thirsty and you gave me no drink, I was a stranger and you did not welcome me, naked and you did not clothe me, sick and in prison and you did not visit me."
>
> Then they also will answer, "Lord, when did we see thee hungry or thirsty or a stranger or naked or sick or in prison, and did not minister to thee?"
>
> Then he will answer them, "Truly, I say to you, as you did it not to one of the least of these, you did it not to me."
>
> And they will go away into eternal punishment, but the righteous into eternal life. (Mt 25:31–46)

There is much that can be said about this parable, and library shelves are overflowing with biblical commentaries, from every mode of the theological spectrum, waxing eloquently on this passage. But doesn't our Lord simply suggest that our entrance one day into His kingdom will depend upon how we have turned our focus away from ourselves onto the needs of the other people in our lives—which is an essential aspect of turning and following either the *Way of Life* or the *Way of Death*? We must begin now to start recognizing the face of Jesus in those around us. This is the avenue along which we will learn true contentment, both now as in the future kingdom, and this involves willfully choosing to seek contentment in our loving care of others.

We left off in our earlier reflection on the Beatitudes with those who have experienced "***purity of heart***" to the extent that they have, by grace, detached themselves from the luring attractions of the world, sin, and themselves. A crisis can arise here, however, through the possibility of isolation. Up to this point, all of the steps of the Beatitudes have the potential of tempting a person into a self-preserving isolation. As a result of our efforts to detach ourselves from the world, sin, and self, followed by a concentrated hunger and thirst for righteousness, and then a desire to be loving and merciful to whoever might cross our path, we may in actuality have cornered ourselves into an exodus from the world, an inward focusing upon ourselves; even a resentful privatization of our spiritual lives, leading to bitterness whenever anyone has the "insensitive gall" to interfere, to intrude upon our "superior" efforts at holiness!

Or, we can respond malleably to the implications and the call of the first six Beatitudes, following in obedience their trajectory out from ourselves, following the example of Christ, out into the world, leading to the next Beatitude: "***Blessed are the peacemakers***." This does not so much mean becoming a skilled negotiator or arbiter between warring peoples, but rather being a willing messenger of Jesus into the lives of others—to be a channel of His peace to others. The reward for stepping out in obedience to live out the implications of these steps in the relationships that God has given us—in our marriages, families, neighborhoods, parishes, workplaces, et cetera—is that people may recognize us as indeed "***sons of God***." They may be moved to "see our good works and give glory to God the Father" (Mt 5:16).

However, they may not, and this can bring about a crisis, which is maybe the primary reason so many of us grow self-focused —especially elderly folk like myself! The others in our lives may react negatively to our efforts, maybe even turning against us in ridicule or persecution. We can respond by backing off; we can return to the safety of our self-focused corner to seek holiness in isolation. Or worse, we can begin doubting, even rejecting the previous stages, giving in to the criticism of the crowd by joining their ranks. We can begin desiring their acceptance over the desire for righteousness, until we have stepped so far backwards that we are once again attached to seeking what is "best" for ourselves, to sin, and to the world.

Or, by grace, we can accept the suffering that comes from reaching out and standing up for what is right and good, pure and true—seeking to help others to learn and grow in true contentment, even if they don't want us to—which leads to the last

Beatitude: "***Blessed are those who are persecuted for righteousness' sake. … Blessed are you when men revile you and persecute you and utter all kinds of evil against you falsely on my account.***" Those who react in ridicule, revile, and even persecute us may not realize why we are reaching out; they may merely be reacting against our pointing out, even if done in love, their failure to do what is true, good, and pure.

Or, by grace, we can accept this rejection as nothing more than what is to be expected and accepted for a follower of Jesus Christ, for which our Lord calls us to "***rejoice and be glad,***" for our true contentment is eternal union with Christ in heaven.

This interpretation of the Beatitudes has a practical application for helping us make more time for others, especially when doing so requires restoring broken relationships. When we experience a broken relationship, with a spouse, family member, or friend, the Beatitudes can provide a step-by-step path towards reconciliation:

> 1st: Humbly recognize that everything we have is a gift of God (gratitude);
>
> 2nd: Recognize our own guilt for sins and the misuse of God's gifts (remorse);
>
> 3rd: Recognize our own pride, which exacerbates difficulties in the relationship (humility);
>
> 4th: Do what is right in the eyes of God (righteousness);
>
> 5th: Turn the other cheek (relinquish the "right to justice" and show mercy);
>
> 6th: Pursue purity of soul and the grace to stand without blemish before God;
>
> 7th: Take action to restore peace, in imitation of God;
>
> 8th: Stand firm in the face of whatever rejection may come for acting according to God's commands, accepting without retaliation ridicule for our faith in Christ.

This may seem idealistic, even insurmountable, but again, like learning and growing in contentment, it is a process empowered by grace through faith. Reconciliation begins with ourselves: setting our hearts and minds in the direction of reconciliation then shapes our prayer, until it sets our convictions and our will, until we step out and make peace with family, friends, and neighbors.

Maybe the simplest way to sum up this long chapter is by the following four principles:

1. Love the Lord your God with all your heart, soul, mind, and strength;
2. Love your neighbor as yourself;
3. Take joy in all the gifts God has given you; and
4. Grasp hold of as little as possible.

9

Make More Time For God

Given all the challenging steps suggested above, maybe now it's time to consider that which is most important: making more time to slow down, wait, pray, and listen to God. Not that we should wait until we've completed the previous steps before embarking on this one—far from it! Rather, making time for Him is our perennial duty, and the previous steps each can facilitate this.

I've come to see that the main thing we have lost as a society and as individuals, in unapologetically accepting the modernist belief in progress and all of its effects, is our ability to slow down, wait on the Lord, and listen quietly for His voice.

Just think about how far and fast, in just the past few decades, our world has descended down the modernist, progressive path. How, as a culture, we are even less able to slow down, wait on the Lord, and listen quietly. How the freed-up time, talents, and energy we, as a culture, have reaped from our unexamined addictions to every new technology have been redirected into such meaningless, time-consuming activities, and too often into unanticipated, often immoral choices and lifestyles. And the entanglements we have brought upon ourselves, and our families, are almost impossible to break. Just think about how much money most of us spend every month on entertainment and communication services that twenty-five years ago we never even imagined having, let alone financing. Of course, for most of us, the impact of these expenditures is assuaged because we've set them up as automatic withdrawals—we don't even need to expend time, energy, and effort in paying for our entanglements.

So, what's the answer? Well, that's personal, of course, and given my own record, I'm hardly the one to give advice. But I think at least one answer can be found somewhere in our efforts to break free, so that we can once again—or maybe for the first time in our lives—slow down, wait on the Lord, and listen to Him quietly. Didn't our Lord Himself encourage His disciples, "But when you pray, go into your room and shut the door and pray to your Father who is in secret; and your Father who sees in secret will reward you" (Mt 6:7)?

Are there ways in which we can become closer to the means of grace that God has provided through His creation, but most especially through His Church? Merely saying "Thank You, Lord" and acknowledging Him in even the most menial task can turn that task into a powerful channel of grace and peace (cf. Phil 4:6, 7). Do you have a place in your life where you can "shut the door" away from the distractions of the world and the entanglements and enticements of modern technology, or are you so entangled that you can't even imagine life without them anymore?

The Apostle John ended his First Letter very abruptly. Without any semblance of a salutation or conclusion, he simply wrote, "Little children, keep yourselves from idols" (1 Jn 5:21). Maybe this was because there was nothing more significant he could have said: anything in our lives that distracts us from God—from seeing His fingerprints and creative love in the world around us—can become an idol. Have the enticing modern technologies, which have made our modern world run so smoothly and efficiently, and have filled our lives with leisure and made our muscles and minds too flabby to exert ourselves in anything creative or challenging—have these entanglements become our new idols? Lord, help us to keep ourselves from them, to use them for the purposes You intended, to free ourselves from the things to which we have already become impotently entangled, so that we can prevent our children and grandchildren from becoming as entangled as we.

By recognizing and accepting the beauty of the very spot where God has placed us right now; by thanking Him for the people He has put right now into our lives; by focusing on that which is more stable, and not forever moving and elusive; by opening our eyes to the vestiges of God everywhere in the world around us; by shutting our minds to the thousands of conflicting, clamoring voices inundating us from all sides; by choosing to make steps toward a life of gospel simplicity; by freeing ourselves from the clutching control and anxieties of debt and unsure investments; by looking for ways to practice a spirit of poverty and detachment; and by constantly turning our focus away from ourselves to the needs of others—by focusing on all these things, we can become freer to commune with God in prayer; to meditate on His Word in Scripture; to hear His voice in liturgy; to receive His grace and forgiveness—His very self—in the sacraments; and to recognize the fingerprints of His love in nature; and then more effectively, by grace, we can become the persons He created in His Image.

Godliness with Contentment

Saint Paul made an interesting statement about contentment in his first letter to his novice bishop Timothy, who had been assigned to lead the Church at Ephesus. Near the close of the letter, after conveying an invaluable list of helpful pastoral advice, he writes:

> There is great gain in godliness with contentment. (1 Tim 6:6)

At first glance, it sounds like Paul is talking about the important connection between godliness, or holiness, and an attitude of contentment. And, yes, I think this is crucially true, but I would humbly suggest that, in this case, this may not be the point Paul was trying to make. To mine the gold of this short but rich statement, we'll need to dig a bit deeper.

First, the Greek term translated as "with" in this sentence denotes "a close connection between two nouns, upon the first of which the emphasis lies."[31] I found this clarification significant: growing in godliness and contentment are interconnected and both important—I don't think a person can really have one without the other—but godliness is the noun "upon the first of which the emphasis lies." In other words, of the two, godliness is the more important. I hate to make distinctions here, but I believe Saint Paul is suggesting, in essence, that in the big scheme of things, when one day we stand before God, the extent of our *godliness* will be more important than the level of our *contentment.*

So, let's consider what Saint Paul might be meaning here by *godliness.* More often than not, commentators and even many translators interpret *godliness* as essentially just another way of saying *holiness* or *righteousness.* This is not a bad thing, since growing in holiness and righteousness is essential, both in this life and in preparation for the next, for, as the author of Hebrews warned, without "holiness … no one will see the Lord" (see Heb 12:14).

However, the word *godliness* here, as well as its few other appearances in the New Testament, can mean something much more significant. The word *godliness* comes from a Greek word (εὐσέβεια) that is very rare in the New Testament, found only in Paul's pastoral epistles and the second letter of Peter. It's a contraction of two words: εὐ, which means "good," and σέβεια, which means "worship" or "reverent respect."[32] Essentially, therefore, *godliness* literally means "good worship" or, as some translators have it, "piety" or "religion." For example, in Paul's Second Letter to Timothy, when he warns what the last days will be like, after compiling a list of human depravities (disturbingly descriptive of today), he adds that men will be "holding the form of *religion* but denying the power of it" (2 Tim 4:5). The Greek term here translated "religion" is the same term used elsewhere for *godliness;* in other words, it could be translated, "holding the form of *godliness* but denying the power of it." (It's significant to note that immediately after this, Paul adds, "Avoid such people.")

The term *godliness,* therefore, does not so much refer to a person's quality of character, like holiness or righteousness, but to how he worships God. In the context of the *Two Ways* I discussed earlier, *godliness* essentially refers to the extent to which a person has turned to face God with his entire being.

I would suggest that the appearance of an even rarer word in the New Testament confirms this. Earlier in First Timothy, Paul writes, "women should adorn themselves modestly and sensibly in seemly apparel, not with braided hair or gold or pearls or costly attire but by good deeds, as befits women ***who profess religion***" (1 Tim 2:9–10). The word *religion* here translates the rare Greek term θεοσέβειαν, which is a contraction of θεο, meaning "God", and σέβειαν, which, as before, means "worship." In some translations, this appears as *godliness,* but again, the point is that here we are dealing not with a woman's quality of character but with how she expresses her worship of God.

Since both terms, *piety* and *religion*, today carry a heft of negative baggage depending upon one's spiritual experience, I'm going to focus on the simpler, more literal meaning of *godliness* as *good worship*. To see how this clarifies its meaning, let's look at the few other places where this term is used in the New Testament:

> Great indeed, we confess, is the mystery of our ***good worship***: He was manifested in the flesh, vindicated in the Spirit, seen by angels, preached among the nations, believed on in the world, taken up in glory. (1 Tim 3:16)

> Have nothing to do with godless and silly myths. Train yourself in ***good worship***; for while bodily training is of some value, ***good worship*** is of value in every way, as it holds promise for the present life and also for the life to come. (1 Tim 4:7,8)

> If any one teaches otherwise and does not agree with the sound words of our Lord Jesus Christ and the teaching which accords with ***good worship*** … he knows nothing ... wrangling among men who are depraved in mind and bereft of the truth, imagining that ***good worship*** is a means of gain. … But as for you, man of God, shun all this; aim at righteousness, ***good worship***, faith, love, steadfastness, gentleness. (1 Tim 6:3,5,11)

> Paul, a servant of God and an apostle of Jesus Christ, to further the faith of God's elect and their knowledge of the truth which accords with ***good worship*** … (Titus 1:1)

> His divine power has granted to us all things that pertain to life and ***good worship***, through the knowledge of him who called us to his own glory and excellence … (2 Ptr 1:3)

> For this very reason make every effort to supplement your faith with virtue, and virtue with knowledge, and knowledge with self-control, and self-control with steadfastness, and steadfastness with ***good worship***, and ***good worship*** with brotherly affection, and brotherly affection with love. (2 Ptr 1:5–7)

> Since all these things are thus to be dissolved, what sort of persons ought you to be in lives of holiness and ***good worship*** … (2 Ptr 3:11)

Some of you may find the sound of these verses awkward, if you're more accustomed to reading *godliness* as *holiness* or *righteousness*, but, as illustrated by the last verse from Second Peter, there is a distinction between *holiness* and *godliness*. What we're talking about here is the importance of good, true worship, or as Paul warns against: practicing a form of good and true worship but denying or ignoring the power of it. In other words, *godliness* or *good worship*, does not consist of empty rituals, or mindless, repeated prayers and liturgies, or the mere passing along the conveyor belt of the Church's sacramental life. This is precisely what Paul was warning against: displaying an *external* show of *good worship* while denying or just being oblivious to the power that is truly present in worship, in the rituals, and in the sacraments.

This is because at the core, the word *godliness* or *good worship* means more than just giving homage. In its most rudimentary sense it implies standing back in awe. In essence, to grow in *godliness* means to grow in awe of God. Essentially *godliness* is a New Testament word that parallels the Old Testament call to *fear God. Godliness* or *good worship* is not, therefore, so much about us; *godliness* is always about Him, about growing in awe of Him, stepping back and recognizing that by the mercy of God's grace we have been awakened to the fact that we are standing in the very presence of the Creator of the Universe. To walk through the steps of our liturgical worship without this underlying core of awe is an empty sham—and, sadly, an empty sham that is presently running rampant amongst both Catholic Christians and non-Catholic Christians. Growing in *godliness* is about becoming more and more and more about Him in every aspect of our lives.

So, can you see how essential *contentment* is to *godliness*, to *good worship*, and why *good worship* in awe of God our Creator is of the first importance in learning contentment? This is why I think Saint Paul made this particular warning to Saint Timothy:

> Teach and urge these duties. If any one teaches otherwise and does not agree with the sound words of our Lord Jesus Christ and the teaching which accords with ***good and true worship*** he is puffed up with conceit, he knows nothing; he has a morbid craving for controversy and for disputes about words, which produce envy, dissension, slander, base suspicions, and wrangling among men who are depraved in mind and bereft of the truth, imagining that [good worship] is a means of gain. (1 Tim 6:2b–5)

A constant problem that Saint Paul and the other apostles were increasingly facing was the rise of seemingly faithful teachers who, however, were teaching things contrary to what the apostles taught. To combat this, Paul insisted that they hold to (1) "the sound words of our Lord Jesus Christ"—in other words, what was found in the Gospels and Apostolic oral tradition, and (2) "the teaching that accords with *good worship*"—which, therefore, refers to the liturgical worship passed on and practiced since the beginning.

The earliest description we have of Christian worship is in Acts 2:

> And they devoted themselves to the apostles' teaching and fellowship, to the breaking of bread and the prayers. And ***fear*** came

> upon every soul; and many wonders and signs were done through the apostles. And all who believed were together and had all things in common; and they sold their possessions and goods and distributed them to all, as any had need. (Acts 2:42–45)

What I find fascinating here is that in this first gathering we observe "*good worship* with contentment." This first gathering of converts sought by grace to humbly and unselfishly obey "the sound words of our Lord Jesus Christ" that He had taught in his *Sermon on the Mount*. And fear or awe (*godliness*) entered the hearts of all gathered. We also observe "the form of *good worship* <u>without</u> denying the power of it"!

The documents of the New Testament record little of the specifics of early Church worship, but we do hear in Hebrews that already many Christians were becoming lax and no longer practicing the early austere worship:

> Let us hold fast the confession of our hope without wavering, for he who promised is faithful; and let us consider how to stir up one another to love and good works, *not neglecting to meet together, as is the habit of some*, but encouraging one another, and all the more as you see the Day drawing near. (Heb 10:23–25)

Going back to Paul's statement, I'd like to suggest that what we hear here is a description of what led to the countless divisions amongst Christians almost from day one of the Church. It was almost as if, with Paul giving this warning, he gave the devil the very strategy he would use in his attempt to destroy God's plan of salvation. For Paul's words are a disheartening description of the battles over words, doctrines, and liturgical practice that have plagued the Church even to this day: "a morbid craving for controversy and for disputes about words, which produce envy, dissension, slander, base suspicions, and wrangling among men".

What is most evident on any Sunday morning in churches all around the world today is the near-infinite variety and disjunction of modes of worship. One finds little effort in following any trustworthy historical teaching on *good worship*; instead, the most prevalent characteristics of modern worship are innovation and freedom. And dare I say there is also little evidence, especially in the modern independent "megachurches," of anyone being concerned about following "the sound words of our Lord Jesus Christ" as expressed in His *Sermon on the Mount*.

Paul's next statement to Timothy, however, is, in fact, an insistence on the sound words of Jesus in His *Sermon*:

> There is great gain in *good worship* with contentment *for we brought nothing into the world, and we cannot take anything out of the world; but if we have food and clothing, with these we shall be content*. But those who desire to be rich fall into temptation, into a snare, into many senseless and hurtful desires that plunge men into ruin and destruction. For the love of money is the root of all evils; it is through this craving that some have wandered away from the faith and pierced their hearts with many pangs. (1 Tim 6:6–10)

Most of what Paul says here confirms what I've tried to address throughout this book, but I think in this context, Paul is trying to say how important true *contentment*, built upon simplicity and detachment, is to true and *good worship*.

As I conclude this chapter on making more time for God, I think it's important that I add a disclaimer; in fact, the same one that Saint Paul gave:

> Not that I have already obtained this or am already perfect; but I press on to make it my own, because Christ Jesus has made me his own. (Phil 3:12)

I am very much in the process of growing in *good worship* with *contentment*, but my wife and I together have fully welcomed the Church's guidance on making both *good worship* and *contentment* a priority in our lives. So, pray for us, and we will pray for you.

10

So, Now What?

Sir Arthur Conan Doyle has Sherlock Holmes quip to his fledgling assistant, "When you have eliminated the impossible, whatever remains, however improbable, must be the truth." As I said in the introduction to this book, this exercise in learning contentment began as a self-reflection, as I struggled with a feeling of discontent upon entering my self-imposed retirement. Admittedly, the underlying question I posed every morning when I dragged myself out of bed and stumbled into the kitchen to make coffee was "Okay, if I'm retired, what am I going to do now?"

This feeling of discontentment drove me to consider all the alternative answers addressed so far in this book. And frankly, by God's mercy and grace, my wife and I have already worked through most of these nine options:

1. We're very contented in our rural home and know that moving somewhere else would not be the answer to any fleeting lack of contentment;

2. As a song said that was popular when we were married, we are very happy "to be stuck with" each other out here in our woods;

3. I've now for years become more than content in the established stability of our beautiful rural setting rather

than the "hustle and bustle" of any of our local "urban jungles";

4. And it's become almost second nature to see the evidence of God and His merciful care in this natural environment.

5. I've long since made choices to reduce the many voices tempting me to seek contentment elsewhere,

6. And over these past twenty-five-plus years, we've made many steps toward simplifying our life together, which most importantly involved adopting attitudes of simplicity.

7. By God's generosity we've made many decisions that have allowed us to now face the future debt free.

8. All of this has been guided by a growing reflection on the call to a poverty of spirit, though I especially have a long way to grow,

9. And by God's mercy, much of this process has been driven by a desire to make more time for Him.

So, if I've eliminated all the alternatives to solving my feelings of discontent, what now am I actually going to do with myself? I will admit that, like many "retired" men, especially those who've stepped down voluntarily, I've been tempted to renege on my decision to retire and reclaim my position of leadership.

I'm reminded of a scene from the comedic movie *Young Frankenstein* when Dr. Frankenstein is about to pass through a rotating wall into a closed cell with the Monster he has created. He turns to his cohorts and dramaticly proclaims, "Now, after I go through, securely shut the door, and under no circumstance open it! Do you understand! Under no circumstance whatsoever open this door!" His cohorts reluctantly agree, the scientist bravely enters, they close and bolt the door, and then they wait. After about five seconds, once the Monster has turned and grunted, the brave scientist quickly looses his resolve and begins screaming, "Let me out! I was only kidding! Open this door!!!" There are days I feel like going back to the office and declaring, "Hey, gang, I was only kidding! Boy, it's good to be back in the saddle," as my former staff members would surely wonder among themselves, "How many times a week is he going to keep doing this?"

I think one of the reasons so many of us in our "twilight years" struggle with discontentment is that, through retirement, we've left behind everything we've been building our contentment upon for the majority of our adult years. Amazingly, as I look back, I think I've been getting up nearly every morning of my life and going somewhere away from home since I started kindergarten at age five! Is this true of you? It's no wonder it takes so long for many retirees to get comfortable with getting up each morning with nowhere specific to go or anything specific to do.

I know of an elderly farmer, God rest his soul, who literally farmed his entire life, from essentially the moment he popped from his mother's womb. In fact, he was born in the very house that he lived in his entire life, and the two hundred plus acres upon which he raised sheep and chickens, milked cows, and harvested apples, pears, and peaches surrounded this very house. Though his life had the usual ups and downs spanning almost the entire twentieth century, he gave no signs of any sense of discontentment in his life of farming.

But when he reached ninety-three, all of his remaining siblings and extended family insisted that it was time for him to slow down, to give up farming, and start "enjoying Life." So, under their pressure, he reluctantly "retired." In less than a year, he was dead.

Most concluded that with the reduction of activity that had always kept him fit, his body just gave out. But I think there was more to this. For all of his life, living in that very house, he would wake up every morning and walk out onto the fields or into the barn and onto his tractor, to do that which not only gave him great pleasure, but upon which his entire understanding of himself was based. He had learned contentment as a farmer, with no desire to do anything else with his life. But now he no longer had the same reasons to get up in the morning. And the fields outside his door were no longer his to care for; the orchards, the sheep, and the farm equipment, which remained all around him, were no longer his responsibility, no longer his to love. He seemed to become withdrawn, and soon he was gone.

I won't presume to suggest that I know better than this old farmer's children, siblings, or extended family what he should or could have done differently. I believe that not a one of us dies before our time, so whenever anyone presumes to have all the answers for the timing and cause of anyone's death, they're just guessing. I remember reading a science fiction story titled "How to Serve Man." An alien had landed on earth and in time had convinced the entire world, through his demonstration of seemingly limitless power, that he was bringing peace and prosperity to everyone! And now he was inviting as many people as wanted to fly away and visit his far-off virtual paradise of a planet. From all around the world, people flocked to get in line for their turn to walk up the steps into his fleet of space transports for the "flight of a lifetime"! But then a scholar translated the title of a book the alien had "accidentally" left behind at one of his talks. The title was "How to Serve Man," and at first this helped convince everyone that the alien had, in fact, come to serve and bring betterment to all of Mankind. But then the scholar was able to translate the book's contents and discovered, to his horror, that the book was a cookbook! He began desperately warning everyone not to get on the transports, for they were, in fact, flying away to the alien planet to be their food—they were willingly crowding into line to become livestock! But no one would listen, for they had become convinced that leaving this crazy world and flying to the alien's supposed paradise was the best possible option for their lives.

Well, the exact opposite is true in our world: every one of us does everything possible to keep from leaving this crazy world, from dying, to live as long as possible on this planet, when, in fact, our eventual departure from life in this world is potentially one of the best things that will ever happen to any of us. This, of course, depends upon many things, as I've discussed throughout this book—and it's certainly possible for many that the departure from this life may not mean they are heading towards that "better place" they have always presumed was their automatic destination. Nonetheless, departing from this life is not an option any of us can avoid. It may come sooner or later than any of us expect, but our destination is fully, by grace, our individual decision, and by grace within our grasp.

"What, then, am I going to do now?" I fear too many discontented men and women in their twilight years put too much of their focus on trying to regain whatever contentment they once had in this temporary world, when, in fact, most of us have been given the greatest of gifts: with fewer responsibilities, and with limited physical endurance to be tempted to spend all our remaining years pursuing mindless distractions, we can now dedicate more of our time to doing the very things upon which true contentment can be achieved—which are, in fact, the things that best prepare us for the eternal journey that awaits us all.

In the years leading up to his assignment as the bishop of Hippo in North Africa, Saint Augustine expressed in a letter to his friend Nebridius the ideal towards which they should abide: *deificari in otio*, which Peter Brown translates as "grow god-like in their retirement." This phrase can also be translated "grow god-like in leisure," which may be more in line with what Augustine was trying to convey at his age.

But I think either translation applies: Have the ways we've spent our leisure moments throughout our lives drawn us closer to God, changing us by grace to become more god-like, or have our "down" times drawn us down? Well, especially now in our retirement, we have the gift of time, leisure time, to focus our attention and efforts on following Saint Paul's instructions: "put off the old nature" and by grace "put on the new":

> *Put off your old nature* which belongs to your former manner of life and is corrupt through deceitful lusts, and be renewed in the spirit of your minds, and *put on the new nature*,

> created after the likeness of God in true righteousness and holiness. (Eph 4:22–24)
>
> *Put to death therefore what is earthly in you*: immorality, impurity, passion, evil desire, and covetousness, which is idolatry. On account of these the wrath of God is coming. In these you once walked, when you lived in them. But now put them all away: anger, wrath, malice, slander, and foul talk from your mouth. Do not lie to one another, seeing that you have *put off the old nature* with its practices and have *put on the new nature*, which is being renewed in knowledge after the image of its creator. (Col 3:5–10)

Fortunately, there is one thing I know about that old retired farmer I just described: after "retirement," when he got up each morning and went outside with coffee in hand, looking out at the fields, barn, and livestock that represented the focus of his entire life, the truth is that his focus was not downward. He didn't spend his final days moping, focused on all that he used to do; rather, his focus was upward, grateful to God, who had given him the great privilege of living his entire life out there on that hilly, rugged farm, upon which his contentment had always been based. He had always been a man of faith, and his final year was not a year of regret, but one of gratitude, waiting and watching for the time when His Lord would come again, for him, to take him home.

I'm hesitant to add this because, to many of you, it may just sound corny, but thinking of this fine old farmer reminded me of a song that was popular when I was a child, sung by actor Walter Brennan. This country ballad, "Old Rivers," concluded:

> Now, one of these days I'm gonna climb that mountain, walk up there among them clouds, where the cotton's high and the corn's a-growin' and there ain't no fields to plow. With the sun beating down across the fields I see that mule, Old Rivers, and me.[33]

I hope someday to have the contentment I saw in the eyes and smile of that good old farmer.

So, where is your focus? On all the things of your past that you miss, or the things you wish you would have done? On the things that once made you content, or maybe you thought would have made you content if you had been able to acquire them? If this is your focus, then you might be missing the most important gift God has given you in this final chapter of your life.

In essence, I would suggest that maybe it's time for us to make a concerted effort to start living all those things we've been preaching at others all of our lives—or maybe to start living the very things others have been trying to teach us, but in our stubbornness, we've refused to listen.

1. **How we loved God**. This is summarized in what is called the *Great Commandment*: "You shall love the Lord your God with all your heart, and with all your soul, and with all your mind, and with all your strength" (Mk 12:30). How grateful were we to the Father through Jesus Christ by the power of the Holy Spirit, for all that He has given us, which means everything, every opportunity to know, love, and serve Him?

In his classic autobiography of faith, *The Seven Storey Mountain*, Thomas Merton described the Trappist monastery where he would spend the rest of his life as a "school in which we learn from God how to be happy." As I suggested in chapter one of this book, unless God calls you to leave the world to become a Trappist, as He did for Merton, I don't believe God requires that we radically change our location or living circumstances in order to at least begin to learn and grow in contentment. For that reason, I believe the rest of what Merton describes applies also to those of us outside the monastery walls:

> Our happiness consists in sharing the happiness of God, the perfection of His unlimited freedom, the perfection of His love. What has to be healed in us is our true nature, made in the likeness of God. What we have to learn is love. The healing and the learning are the same thing, for at the very core of our essence we are constituted in God's likeness by our freedom, and the exercise

> of that freedom is nothing else but the exercise of disinterested love—the love of God for his own sake, because He is God.[34]

From the perspective of the *Two Ways* mentioned earlier, to love God is to turn all that we are, all of our senses, fully in His direction. The mystery is that this is also what it means to *fear* Him, as well as *love* Him. When we think of loving our Creator God and Father, it is important that we hear the full context from which our Lord Jesus quoted the Great Commandment:

> And now, Israel, what does the LORD your God require of you, but to fear the LORD your God, to walk in all his ways, to love him, to serve the LORD your God with all your heart and with all your soul, and to keep the commandments and statutes of the LORD, which I command you this day for your good? (Deut 10:12–13)

2. **How we loved.** This is the second Great Commandment: "You shall love your neighbor as yourself," and our Lord added, "There is no other commandment greater than these" (Mk 12:31).

When all the great industrialists, bankers, inventors, philanthropists, and investors die, what will ultimately matter will not be all the great things they made, accumulated, and accomplished, for all that will stay in the box, left behind in this world. Rather, what will matter is how they loved their wives, children, families, friends, and neighbors, as well as the people they worked with. As Thomas à Kempis wrote: "Without love, the outward work is of no value; but whatever is done out of love, be it ever so little, is wholly fruitful. For God regards the greatness of the love that prompts a man, rather than the greatness of his achievement."[35]

This, too, will be the measure of our lives. As Saint Francis of Assisi once said, "Men lose all the material things they leave behind them in this world, but they carry with them the reward of their charity and the alms they give. For these they will receive from the Lord the reward and recompense they deserve."[36]

3. **How we indirectly loved**. How did the way we spent our money, invested our time, and applied our talents affect other people in this world, people we didn't even know? If our ambition for power, position, prosperity, and wealth caused us to step on even one person, I believe that when the books are opened in the end, and everything we have done in this life is examined, that person will be there in the judgment, pointing, as Nathan did to David, and saying, "You are the man!" (2 Sam 12:7).

How many people around the world, whom we will never know personally, have been affected by how we have spent our money, by what we have said, or by what we have done in this life? Or maybe what we haven't but should have done?

4. **How we grew in grace.** What have we learned about ourselves, if we were listening, and how have we responded? How have we changed? Or have our lives been one continual disclaimer that we were without faults (cf. 1 Jn 1:8) or that it was always someone else's fault? As Saint Paul warned, "Put to death what is earthly in you …" (Col 3:5f.).

To some extent, the Scriptures from beginning to end can be seen as one continuous call to grow in grace, or holiness. Jesus said that the central commandments for His followers were to love God and one another. The rest of the New Testament is essentially about how to live this out. Holiness, therefore, is how we live out our loving of God with heart, mind, soul, and strength, with the living visible people in our lives as the primary recipients.

Lots of things can distract us from growing in grace. Jesus once warned his potential disciples that "no one who puts his hand to the plow and looks back is fit for the kingdom of God" (Lk 9:62). Sometimes it's the suffering, sadness, frustration, discouragement, radical changes in course, or even failures that remain or even seem to increase after we've chosen to put our hands to the plow that distract us from following and serving Christ.

Maybe we are most distracted, though, by our vanity: wondering whether anyone is watching, admiring, and praising our progress and accomplishments. The more we become caught up in this, the more the plow swerves, and the less fit we have become "for the kingdom of God."

Have you ever heard of the term *entropy*? *Merriam-Webster Dictionary* defines *entropy* as "the degradation of the matter and energy in the universe to an ultimate state of inert uniformity." More simply, entropy measures the usual movement in nature of order to disorder. Without the input of energy to establish and maintain order, everything in nature moves toward disorder (and this can be scientifically proven by looking into any adult male's sock drawer).

This is also a God-given illustration of "spiritual entropy." If we neglect to take time to examine the state of our soul, to repent, pray, worship, meditate on God's Word, and to love, this neglect will become the state of our soul. As the great Dominican theologian Réginald Garrigou-Lagrange once said, "In the way of God, he who makes no progress loses ground."[37] We never in this life reach a safe plateau where we can presume we have spiritually arrived. If we are not growing in our relationship with God the Father through His Son Jesus Christ, by the power of the Holy Spirit, we are dying—we are "losing ground."

Saint Paul's *Letter to the Ephesians* is all about this. Paul was writing to Christians who had been saved by grace through faith from their former pagan way of life (see 2:8). As I mentioned earlier, He exhorted them to continue, even though "saved," to "[p]ut off your old man which belongs to your former manner of life and is corrupt through deceitful lusts, and be renewed in the spirit of your minds, and put on the new man, created after the likeness of God in true righteousness and holiness" (4:22–24).

I remember hearing a story about a tourist driving across Scotland, admiring the rolling farmlands, until one particularly beautiful and abundant garden stopped him in his tracks. He got out of his car to admire the well-kept and bountiful rows of vegetables. As he approached, the Scottish gardener suddenly popped up into view from behind an enormous berry bush. The tourist exclaimed, "My, God has blessed you with a beautiful garden!"

To that, the Scottish gardener replied, "Ach! You shoulda seen it when God had it to His lonesome!"

Without the willful input of energy and effort through the aid of grace, our spiritual lives can quickly move from order to disorder.

By grace, we generally do not regress spiritually all the way back to our "former way of life"—that is, if we regularly reexamine the purpose, the state, the boundaries, and the order in our lives. However, if we have forgotten or never taken the time to consider the reason God created us and placed us into this world, if we have neglected the nurturing of our mind and heart, if we have become negligent in maintaining adequate boundaries around our senses and person, and therefore our conscience and soul, we likely have allowed our lives to drift into seemingly paralyzing disorder.

We can, nonetheless, clear-cut the weeds, brambles, and junk trees from our lives; we can reestablish the boundaries; we can reestablish order; and we can remember and recommit ourselves to the very purpose for which we were created. All it takes is contrition, repentance, and recommitment to Him who knew each of us before we were even formed in the womb. All of this is possible through prayer and the graces God gives us.

So, as you read these words, how content are you? Jesus told His followers to "*abide in my love* … [so] that my joy may be in you, and that your joy may be full" (Jn 15:10,11). When our lives are over and we look back, will we see that our lives were full of the joy of Christ, or of anxiety, bitterness, ingratitude, and regret?

Let me address something that is certainly possible if not probable. Even if we are able, by grace, to do everything I've suggested in this book, there will always come times when something or someone will bring frustration or anger or bitterness into our lives, and therefore, a sense of discontentment. Or, we'll remember something from the past that dredges up these same feelings of discontentment, or maybe the fear of what lies ahead will start to poison everything we've accomplished by grace. So, now what?

I believe more and more that what is most important is not anything about our past, or about where we might be or what we might have in the future, but about how we are being faithful right now, in the present moment, where God has planted us, with whom He has called us to live, with what we have, and what we have been given.

The past is gone. The only element of the past that can become a present necessity is an offense for which we need to make amends or seek forgiveness. This must be fixed if it has been neglected, for otherwise, like an unkept field, it will only grow into an unsurpassable wall of briars.

The future, on the other hand, is but an unfathomable concoction of our efforts and the grace of God. Since we have no way of knowing for certain our future, we can only focus every effort on being humbly obedient in the present moment, knowing that God will work "for good with those who love him, who are called according to his purpose" (Rom 8:28). Or, as my favorite Proverb puts it: "Trust in the Lord with all your heart, and do not rely on your own insight. In all your ways acknowledge him, and he will make straight your paths" (Prov 3:5–6).

Our plans are not always God's plans, but an essential part of learning contentment involves recognizing more and more that His plans are always best. As the great Christian writer C.S. Lewis once said:

> The great thing, if one can, is to stop regarding all the unpleasant things as interruptions of one's "own" or "real" life. The truth is of course that what one calls the interruptions are precisely one's real life—the life God is sending one day by day; what one calls one's "real life" is a phantom of one's own imagination.[38]

Sometimes discontent comes because we have lost the trusting thrill of our present moment. Regardless of our present situation, we too can know that our Creator and Father has nothing but good in store for those who thankfully acknowledge Him in all they do, trusting that by making straight their paths, he will empower them by grace to grow in His likeness.

Allow me to add one more related thought. As far as I know, there are no courses entitled *Growing Old 101*. Besides, most of us would miss most of the lectures, either nodding off or making periodic trips to the *loo*. But there is something I've learned unexpectedly.

Imagine a story written about your family when you were a child. Your parents would most likely be the focal points of the plot, with you and your siblings, if any, colorful and sometimes disruptive subplots, and your grandparents, another more distant subplot. You and your siblings flavor the story, as you live under the authoritative leadership of your parents, and your grandparents make cameo appearances as "extended family."

Now imagine a story written 20–30 years later when you and your spouse (if married) are now the focal points of your family story. The primary plot of your story mostly precedes in response to how you and your spouse are leading; your children, if any, are subplots adding color and, of course, challenging diversions, while your parents have become their own now more distant subplots, as "extended family" making cameo visits.

Now imagine the story being written 30–50 years later. Now your children in the previous story are parents of their own families, with their own stories, in which they are now the focal points. Their children—your grandchildren—are the creative, colorful subplots, and you, well, now you're the more distant subplots, the "extended family," making what cameo appearances you can, dependent upon distance, availability, health, and finances.

This transition from being a child to being a parent to being a grandparent—from being an obedient, submissive "subplot" to being the responsible, authoritative, and wise focal point, to becoming now a more distant subplot, an "extended member of the family"—was, for me, a bit of an unexpected education. *Learning Contentment* involves recognizing that as we grow older, we become less and less the focal points of our own family's story—at least this is more the norm in our twenty-first century world. This is something, however, we must not mourn, but learn to celebrate, and to support with prayer and selfless charity.

So, if we're no longer the focal points of our family, what's our job now? Now we have time and freedom to focus on the one thing necessary: becoming saints. Not necessarily the canonized version with a capital "S" but the kind Saint Paul talked about: putting off the old man and putting on Christ. Then someday, by grace, we can have an even more important subplot in the family story: we can pray for them from heaven, when our egos have been completely transformed.

Imagine having your name for all time in the New Testament as one who was so "in love with this present world" that you abandoned Saint Paul (see 2 Tim 4:10). When our children, grandchildren, and those who knew our deeds and words remember us, will how we lived be a legacy worth imitating?

Saint Paul once warned the Roman Christians, "Besides this you know what hour it is, how it is full time now for you to wake from sleep. For salvation is nearer to us now than when we first believed" (Rom 13:11). In the context of a verse from Hebrews about being "surrounded by so great a cloud of witnesses" (12:1–2), I might suggest that it's high time for us to quit procrastinating and start acting. These *witnesses* are not just the heavenly hosts, angels, martyrs, and saints, who are watching and cheering us on, but our spouses, children, grandchildren, friends, neighbors, co-workers, even the viewers, hearers, and readers of our high-sounding words(!)—all of these are waiting to see whether we actually live out faithfully all of the things we been teaching and preaching all of our lives.

May God grant us the grace and mercy to know, love, and serve Him; to love one another; to consider how our actions and lifestyles affect people we will never know; to grow in holiness; to be content with, yet detached from, a minimum of things; and to leave behind a model for our children and grandchildren to follow, in Christ. Amen.

AUTHOR'S ADDENDUM

Some of you may find some of the material in this short book familiar, so allow me to explain how this book evolved. Twelve years ago, after I'd just turned sixty, I was preparing to speak at a Men's Conference, and a friend asked me what I was going to do when I grew up? After a quick thought, I answered that the first twenty years of my life had been focused on ME; then after a religious awakening in college, the focus of my second twenty years shifted, by grace, to JESUS CHRIST; and then, again by grace, the focus of my third twenty years was on JESUS AND HIS CHURCH. So, what might I do if the Lord blesses me with yet another twenty years of life? I quipped to my friend, "I think it's time for me to start living out all those things I've been preaching to others for the past forty-plus years!"

Later that evening, as I reflected on that comment, a Scripture text ran across my mind like a banner, as maybe the definitive starting point for this next twenty years. It was a statement made by John the Baptist, as his own off-the-cuff comment to a similar conference of men, as he unknowingly faced the final period of his own life. Pointing to Jesus, whom he had just baptized in the Jordon, John told his disciples: "He must increase, but I must decrease" (Jn 3:30).

I quickly found out that the mere verbalization of that personal challenge was an unanticipated invitation to both the Holy Spirit and the devil to up their game in the battle over my soul, like the proverbial picture of an angel and a devil poised on opposing shoulders. Oh, I'm not claiming that the metaphysical battle over my soul sets me apart as anyone special; on the contrary, I was only beginning to experientially appreciate what a vast number of others—maybe a myriad of others, especially those like me in the *twilight years* of life, and maybe you my reader—are also experiencing, and maybe struggling for answers, especially during these difficult "times that try men's souls."

Admittedly, the first twelve years of this next (maybe last) twenty years have not been a piece of cake. Trying to "slow down, wait, and listen to the Lord" has been a bit like going through a detox program. Now my wife and I are empty nesters. We live on what our family has long called "the farm," which is by far a false moniker. Part of taking the call to "decrease" seriously has meant facing up to what I (at best, an unsuccessful "hobby" farmer) can responsibly do with thirty-seven acres of rolling Appalachian foothills, all by myself, at age seventy-three. I've often quipped that I'm just an old second-string college football player trying to keep from looking like a football. Well, I've failed at that, too. So, we've reduced our periodically changing menagerie of dairy cows, beef cattle, sheep, pigs, and chickens down to five partially independent cats.

So, what am I going I do with myself, now that I've "grown up"? By the time I was twelve years into this next twenty, it seemed like it was about time to actually make a succinct list of all those things I've had the audacity to preach to others for the past fifty-plus years. This way, I could truly examine my life, get myself by grace back realigned and fully traveling in the right direction, and then maybe pass a few things along to others, especially those who might also be facing the spiritual challenges of the twilight years.

About the same time as that Men's Conference, I had just published a book titled *Life from Our Land*.[39] With hindsight, I think the title may have been unfortunate, for it seems to have instilled little but confusion on what the book was about, let alone where it ought to be shelved or found in a bookstore or library. The book was not intended as a "how to" book on farming or homesteading, nor as a call to abandon the city and escape to the country, nor as a shout-out for modern environmentalism. Rather, my purpose was to share what we as a family had learned about life, and maybe more importantly, what we had discovered about how we ought to be living our lives, from having the privilege of living out here on our beautiful, mostly wooded land in the Southern Ohio Appalachian foothills.

It then struck me that of all the materials I've published over the years, it was that book, *Life from Our Land*, that most succinctly brought my convictions together. This book, therefore, began as a condensation of that book, from which I extracted and then rearranged, synthesized, and simplified the primary thoughts I had tried to convey, but now without the sometimes "charming" but distracting farming and homesteading anecdotes. I then threw into this mix a few extra articles that had spilled from my pen in the intervening years.

The primary difference between the first book and this newer compilation is the underlying and interconnecting theme. In *Life from Our Land*, I wove together what were originally disconnected articles and blog posts under the umbrella of homesteading and back-to-the-land living. I wasn't so much trying to convince my (few) readers to leave the city and retreat to the land, but rather to recognize some wisdom we had gained from doing this ourselves that they might consider following wherever they might happen to live.

In this newer compilation, maybe because I'm looking back in my twilight years, I found myself surprisingly reshaping and interconnecting the key points under the theme of *Learning Contentment*. Regardless of where a person lives or the situation in which one finds himself, how does he seek and find true contentment? Since contentment is primarily a choice rather than a feeling, much of this book is about learning contentment regardless of one's situation. There are some things, though, we can do to grease the shoots, so to say, to help the rewarding feelings of contentment to follow one's positive choices. Therefore, there is a mixture of both in this book, and I hope my thoughts are as much of an encouragement to you as they continue to be a challenge to me.

As I close these reflections, I need to confess something that has only come to light in the process of editing and re-editing this book. I said in the introduction that the first twenty years of my life were about ME, the second twenty were about JESUS, the third twenty were about JESUS AND HIS CHURCH, and now the last twenty (or so) years were to be about living out all those things I've been preaching to others all my life. The theme of these last years was to be "He must increase, while I must decrease." I just had no idea the extent to which this process would dredge stuff up from the depth of my soul.

I'm discovering something about myself of which I've never been aware—something I would have always denied vociferously, but which, in actuality, I now see was always true. These past seventy-plus years have not really been divided up so cleanly as I creatively suggested. The truth is, my life has, in fact, always been about ME. I'm tempted to wax eloquently into great detail to illustrate how I'm seeing that this has been true from my earliest days of being an only child performing my banjo ukulele in front of my first grade class—but once again, this would only be me waxing eloquently about ME.

I have always preached that our surrender to Jesus Christ requires a complete surrender of Self; that the third Beatitude of "Blessed are the meek" is about growing in selfless humility. Even seemingly centuries ago, as a youth minister, I preached a sermon using three large wooden blocks, painted with the large letters J, O, and Y, to exhort my young congregation that true joy was not spelled YJO (Yourself, Jesus, and then Others) but is spelled JOY (JESUS, OTHERS, and then YOURSELF). I've preached this theme of selfless humility from pulpits, on television and radio, in blog posts, and in print, but I'm only starting to see the extent to which all of my life, in one way or another, has been about being up front "in the limelight." Maybe God used my recent watching of Charlie Chaplin's masterpiece movie *Limelight* to awaken me to this long-standing flaw in my personality.

In all honesty, this has never been my conscious desire or motive. My only desire, for at least the last fifty-plus years, has been to discern God's will and then do it—and by His mercy and generosity, He has opened countless doors for me to serve Him. I'm eternally grateful for this. But in the process, I just unknowingly became more and more accustomed to feeding my ego by being up front. I may have been speaking sincerely about Him, or about His Church, or about our need to turn from ourselves to others, but in fact, I was blindly basking in the attention. Frankly, as I have the audacity to write a book about *Learning Contentment,* I'm finding that the main reason contentment might still be for me so elusive is that I don't know yet how to live without somehow being up front.

I see now that the reason God called me to back down from public ministry was so that, in the time I have remaining, I can learn to let go fully of myself so that I can truly become, by His grace, a channel of His love and mercy to others—no longer from a pulpit "in the limelight," but just to family, friends, and neighbors—I guess another form of practicing "personal subsidiarity" in the *twilight years* of life.

I have no idea to what extent this also might be true for any of you my readers, but all I can say, if I'm allowed to preach at least one more time, is to repeat that the only true way to spell JOY, the only path towards true contentment, is to put JESUS first, OTHERS second, and YOURSELF last. May God in His mercy help us to see the ways we've gotten this backwards, so that, by His grace, we can become channels of His love and mercy, not just in the time we have left on this planet, but right now to the very next person He places in our path.

Appendix 1

How Can We Know What's True?

Jesus said to those who believed in Him, "If you continue in my word, you are truly my disciples, and you will know the truth, and the truth will make you free" (Jn 8:31–32). Unfortunately, now, nearly two thousand years after this promise, the vast majority of the world's population still repeats Pontius Pilate's conundrum: "What is truth?"

Never in the history of the world have the lives of people—elderly, middle-aged, and children—been so inundated with opinions on what is true, particularly not just how we are to live our lives but how we are to understand our very selves. The bookstores and Internet are overflowing with books and blogs by authors who, for example, use examples from Scripture or nature to prove all kinds of things, from Christian truth to Hinduism, Buddhism, New Age, and even atheism; from investment strategies to leadership principles to political platforms to dietary assumptions to parenting ideals to new moral codes. Scripture and nature have been used to justify some of the most radically contradictory ideals, from extreme isolationist pacifism to radical social Darwinism; even to denying the viability of the family, marriage, and monogamous relationships—even to eugenics, infanticide, and genocide.

So, yes, there is truth to be found and there are lessons to be learned by studying Scripture and nature, but how can we be certain that our conclusions are trustworthy and ought to be passed down to our children? How can we be certain that the writers inundating our lives with opinions are not just using examples from Scripture and nature to justify some hidden personal agenda?

At some point, when I was a young man, a switch in my brain turned on, and I began to desire to know, follow, and then proclaim "the truth." In the late sixties, I sought truth and proclaimed what I had found through folk music, and as any of us past seventy might remember, folk music hardly had a consistent and reliable theme!

In the early 1970s, I turned to science and nature and thought I had found trustworthy assurance in scientific materialism. Chemistry, physics, and especially ecology and environmentalism were the underlying truths that I believed could explain and give meaning to life. Save the planet! But in seeking to save the planet, I came to realize that we were ultimately denuding life itself of all meaning. If humanity is nothing but the accidental concoctions of water and chemicals, and meaningless electrical impulses and hormonal passions—and the worst disease that ever-plagued Mother Earth—then truth itself is but a vapor: nothing to be followed let alone proclaimed. As Steve Nicholls admits in his book *Paradise Found*, "Good and evil, fairness and unfairness have no meaning at all in a world shaped by natural selection."[40]

Then, by God's grace and mercy, I rediscovered the faith of my childhood. My heart and mind were changed. I had found a truth worth living and dying for. From then on, I believed truth could be found only through reading the Scriptures, for, as I quoted earlier, our Lord promised, "If you continue in my word, you are truly my disciples, and you will know the truth, and the truth will make you free" (Jn 8:31–32). Until I was forty years old, and ten years an ordained Protestant minister, I never wavered from this conviction. "How can one know what is true? Through the one trustworthy source: the Bible *alone*. Read the Bible every day, pray it, memorize it, know it, and with the help of the Holy Spirit, you will know what is true and necessary for salvation." But does this work?

In seminary, I was taught a process to ensure that what I proclaimed on Sunday mornings would be biblically true, and I diligently followed this process since my ordination. On Monday mornings, I would begin preparation by making a fresh English translation, from Greek or Hebrew, of whatever text I had scheduled for the following Sunday. I'd then fill pages with exegetical study notes and reflections. Once I had arrived at a tentative conclusion of the meaning of the passage, and a rough outline of my thoughts, then and only then would I consult with the row of biblical commentaries on my shelf to ensure that my conclusions were on track.

One day it struck me: I had handpicked every commentary on my shelf, from scholars I liked, whose theologies I agreed with. In other words, I was merely checking my conclusions against people I already agreed with. In essence, I was only checking myself against myself! I had protected myself from any way of discerning whether I was—or they were—wrong.

Then one Sunday morning as I was preaching, it dawned on me that within a thirty-mile radius of my pulpit, there were probably thirty other pastors in thirty other churches who also considered the Bible the sole authority for our faith. The problem was that I knew we were all teaching different, if not contradictory, things—possibly from the same text. Which one of us—if any of us—was preaching *truth*?

As an evangelically minded Presbyterian Calvinist, I believed and preached "once saved, always saved": that once a person accepts Jesus Christ as Lord and Savior, he has arrived; he is saved by grace through faith *alone*, and because he has done nothing to earn salvation, there is likewise nothing he can do to lose it. This, however, was certainly not what the Methodist, Episcopalian, Wesleyan, Nazarene, Seventh-Day Adventist, Vineyard Fellowship, or Pentecostal, let alone Roman Catholic, ministers around me believed or taught.

As I gazed week after week from my pulpit, I knew many of the intimate details of the lives of my congregation, especially my staff. I began to realize that my understanding of Scripture prevented me from challenging any of them to change their lives. Many of them needed to break from debilitating sin—as demanded in Scripture—and even more of them needed to live their faith more radically, but I had no theological grounds to challenge anyone, let alone any real authority to do so. Certainly, in obedience to Scripture, I called them to turn from sin and to Christ, but my harangues merely bounced off the glazed eyes of their presumptions. The Protestant Reformers had essentially truncated the gospel merely to *being* in Christ by faith *alone*; *abiding* in Christ and *loving* in Christ, though important ways to demonstrate our faith in gratitude to Christ, were not deemed necessary for salvation.

This impotence was particularly evident in moral and life issues. Our Presbyterian denomination, like most mainline denominations, had gradually and democratically redefined the moral implications of the gospel, leaning more and more in a relativistic and pro-choice direction. Marilyn and I were both decidedly pro-life. She was the director of a crisis pregnancy center, and, more often than not, she found herself working beside Catholics whose views were far more in line with ours. I had also discovered that, through the dues that my congregation and I were paying to the head office of our denomination, we were funding abortions—for the daughters and wives of pro-choice ministers—and there was nothing we could do to stop this.

With this, I knew I could no longer remain a pastor in my particular Presbyterian denomination. So I began reading an encyclopedia of Christian denominations—three hundred pages of all the different Christian traditions in America. One by one, I examined each tradition, and one after another, I rejected them. I found something in the theology or practice of each denomination that I could not accept as *true* according to how I understood Scripture.

I received a phone call from a pastor friend who, in a panic, exclaimed, "Marcus, you can't leave the Presbyterian church! You must remain loyal, even if all the leaders have become heretics and the church is going down in flames: we need the faithful to remain loyal!" And I answered, "If that is true, then why did we leave our last denomination to form this one? And the division before that, and before that, and before that? Why does loyalty to *truth* require that I stand firm here and now in this denomination? Why not move on and form a *truer* church? Because in time, we both know that we would have to move on and form another one, and another one, and another ad infinitum."

You see, the motto of at least my Presbyterian heritage has always been "Reformed and always reforming." The way we reformed was through re-forming, starting one new church after another, until today even a Protestant source admits that there are over thirty thousand individual denominations in the world, growing at the rate of one new denomination every five days![41]

In many ways, the phrase "the verses I never saw" best describes my whole spiritual journey: how from an early age God not only brought into my life the gift of the Scriptures but how, more often than not, I just didn't see them—at least not right away. I was in places where they were preached and taught; I read them, over and over daily; I heard them expounded on television and radio; I experienced them as seminary classmates and I debated and fought over them; I even preached and taught on them myself. But, in far too many ways, it took a while for me to fully hear what God was trying to tell me—at least until it was God's time for me to hear.

Then a friend blindsided me with a Scripture text from Saint Paul that I had never "seen" before:

> I hope to come to you soon, but I am writing these instructions to you so that, if I am delayed, you may know how one ought to behave in the household of God, which is *the Church of the living God, the pillar and bulwark of the truth.* (1 Tim 3:14–15)

This Scripture text, therefore, teaches that the Church is the "pillar and bulwark of the truth." I had never given one thought to the necessity of the *Church* for knowing and discerning "the truth." But if Saint Paul was right, then *which* church? My Presbyterian denomination? But which Presbyterian denomination? My local congregation? Or the Lutheran, Methodist, Baptist, Episcopal, Pentecostal, Vineyard Fellowship, et cetera, et cetera, denominations? Or which branch of these? But surely not the Catholic Church! And besides, as a Calvinist Protestant, I believed that the *true* Church was invisible, consisting of true believers all over the world, the membership of which was known only to God.

At that moment, it struck me: How could an invisible church, known only to God, be the pillar and bulwark of anything?

After many months of study and reflection, it became apparent that the key foundation of our Protestant faith, *sola Scriptura*, was not biblical, nor theologically or philosophically sound; in fact, the very Scriptures we used to defend the foundational doctrine did not teach it. Saint Paul had written that "all scripture is inspired by God and profitable for teaching, for reproof, for correction, and for training in righteousness" (2 Tim. 3:16). But this does not teach that Scripture is the sole authority of our faith; nor does Scripture itself define which books are to be included in this collection of inspired Scriptures.

Another friend pointed out *another* verse I had never "seen," 2 Thessalonians 2:15: "Therefore, brethren, stand fast and hold to the traditions which you were taught, whether by word or our epistle" (NKJV). *Tradition!* This verse spoke of the importance of passing on faithfully the apostolic tradition, which was received primarily through the spoken word and only occasionally through epistles when an apostle could not speak to his people directly.

We Evangelical Protestants denied the trustworthiness of any *tradition* as nothing more than the "traditions of men" (cf. Mk 7:8). Yet the reason there is no church in the world that actually lives out *sola Scriptura* is that every church interprets Scripture through the lens of its own passed-on tradition—the tradition of the founder of its movement. It was this nearly limitless assortment of traditions that has spawned the cacophony of opinions, including my own, coming from pulpits every Sunday.

As a result of my reflections, the Protestant foundation of *sola fide* also began to topple. I never questioned, from the time of my childhood Lutheran catechetical formation, that we are saved by faith *alone*, but another verse I had never taken seriously, James 2:24, got my attention: "You see then that a man is justified by works, and not by faith *only*" (NKJV). This revelation concurred with what I had always known in my conscience to be true: We are not merely "once saved, always saved" through some one-time surrendering statement of faith in Christ; we must live this out by grace for the rest of our lives! Again, as Saint James wrote, "But be doers of the word, and not hearers only, deceiving yourselves" (1:22, NKJV).

I cannot give here a detailed account of how my wife and I came to believe that the Catholic Church is this "pillar and bulwark of the truth."[42] Allow me, however, to focus on the one issue that in the end closed the deal.

Jesus did not merely travel around preaching about the kingdom and encouraging every enthusiastic person who chose to follow Him to teach likewise. Rather, He selected twelve apostles and "gave them authority" (Mt 10:1). In every list of these twelve, the Gospel writers place Simon Peter first (see Mt 10:2), and there was a reason for this. To this first of the apostles, Jesus had said:

> You are Peter [Cephas in Aramaic], and on this rock [Cephas] I will build my Church, and the gates of Hades shall not prevail against it. I will give you the keys of the kingdom of heaven, and whatever you bind on earth shall be bound in heaven, and whatever you loose on earth shall be loosed in heaven. (Mt 16:18-19)

On the night on which Jesus was betrayed by one of His own, He told His apostles, "These things I have spoken to you, while I am still with you. But the Counselor, the Holy Spirit, whom the Father will send in my name, he will teach you all things, and bring to your remembrance all that I have said to you" (Jn 14:25-26). In a general way, this promise cannot be true for every single Christian; otherwise why is there so much disagreement between Spirit-filled Christians over what is *true*? Rather, Jesus was promising this to the men to whom He was directly speaking, His hand-chosen apostles, headed by Peter; that "when the Spirit of truth comes, he will guide you into all the truth (Jn 16:13).

After the trial, Crucifixion, and burial of Jesus, Saint Paul wrote to the Christian believers in the city of Corinth:

> Now I would remind you, brethren, in what terms I preached to you the gospel, which you received, in which you stand, by which you are saved, if you hold it fast—unless you believed in vain. For I delivered to you as of first importance what I also received, that Christ died for our sins in accordance with the Scriptures, that he was buried, that he was raised on the third day in accordance with the Scriptures, and that *he appeared to Cephas [Peter], then to the twelve. Then he appeared to more than five hundred brethren at one time, most of whom are still alive, though some have fallen asleep. Then he appeared to James, then to all the apostles. Last of all, as to one untimely born, he appeared also to me.* (1 Cor 15:1–8)

Here even Saint Paul affirms the primary position of Peter (Cephas), but this quotation also emphasizes why the Christian understanding of nature, of life and death, and of eternity is the most trustworthy: it is founded upon the eyewitness testimony to the risen Christ. The man Jesus, who was crucified for claiming to be the Son of God, has risen from the dead. All of His apostles, except John, died as martyrs for their witness to this fact. John died of old age, yet only after years of exile for his witness to the risen Christ. The key question: Would any person willingly accept brutal martyrdom for something they knew was a lie?

After His death and Resurrection, and before He ascended to the Father, Jesus commissioned His hand-chosen apostolic leaders, upon whom He had breathed the promised Holy Spirit (see Jn 20:21–23), to go forth and make disciples, "baptizing them in the name of the Father and of the Son and of the Holy Spirit, teaching them to observe all that I have commanded you" (Mt 28:19–20). In other words, Jesus taught His apostles, who then, guided by the Holy Spirit, were to pass this teaching on faithfully through preaching. New believers were to be enveloped in the fellowship of the Trinity (see 1 Jn 1:3), the Church, through baptism.

At Pentecost, when the Holy Spirit descended with power upon Jesus' apostles, Simon Peter took his responsibility to heart and preached the first Christian sermon. When his hearers exclaimed, "Brethren, what shall we do?" Peter responded, "Repent, and be baptized every one of you in the name of Jesus Christ for the forgiveness of your sins; and you shall receive the gift of the Holy Spirit" (Acts 2:37-38). Here we see all the elements of the beginning and continuity of the Church: our Lord to His apostles, led by Peter, empowered by the Holy Spirit to proclaim *the Word*, and new converts received into the Church through baptism, themselves empowered by the Spirit to proclaim.

Years later, Saint Paul instructed his apprentice bishop Timothy, "What you have heard from me before many witnesses entrust to faithful men who will be able to teach others also" (2 Tim 2:2). Here we see the authority of Saint Paul, which he had received from Saint Peter (see Gal 1:18–2:10), to appoint and empower other men to protect and pass on the apostolic tradition.

Toward the end of the first century, Saint Clement, the fourth bishop of Rome, wrote a letter to the same Christians in Corinth whom Saint Paul had written to decades before. The forcefulness of this letter itself witnesses to a unique authority of the bishop of Rome over a gathering of believers six hundred miles away in a different country. In this letter, Saint Clement witnessed to this apostolic succession of passing on the truth:

> *The apostles received the Gospel for us from our Lord Jesus Christ, and Jesus Christ was sent from God.* So Christ was from God, and the apostles from Christ. So both came by the will of God in good order. Once they received commands, once they were made confident through the resurrection of our Lord Jesus Christ, and once they were entrusted with God's Word, they went out proclaiming with the confidence of the Holy Spirit that the kingdom of God would come. Preaching in lands and cities, by spiritual discernment, they began establishing their first fruits, who were bishops and deacons for future believers. And

> this was nothing new because for many ages it had been written about bishops and deacons, as Scripture says somewhere, "I will appoint bishops for them in justice and deacons in faith."[43]

Then, toward the end of the second century, Saint Irenaeus, the bishop of Lyons, wrote a set of books entitled *Against Heresies*, in which he gave witness to this continuity of apostolic authority:

> But since it would be too long to enumerate ... the successions of all the churches, we shall confound all those who ... assemble other than where it is proper, by pointing out here the successions of the bishops of the greatest and most ancient Church known to all, founded and organized at Rome by the two most glorious apostles, Peter and Paul, that Church which has the tradition and the faith which comes down to us after having been announced to men by the Apostles. *For with this Church, because of its superior origin, all Churches must agree, that is, all the faithful in the whole world*; and it is in her that the faithful everywhere have maintained the Apostolic tradition.[44]

* * *

This chapter is not meant to be a thorough apologetic for the truth of the Catholic Church, nor even a minimal attempt to answer all the objections one might raise against this claim—for the bitter opinions out there against Catholics and the Catholic Church are myriad. Rather, this is merely a way of addressing the big question of where I have come to believe a person can go to find a trustworthy source of authority and wisdom, whether we're trying to interpret the meaning of Scripture or of nature or the meaning of life. This book is but a sampling of why Marilyn and I have never questioned our decision to come home to the Church established by Christ in His apostles, centered on the authority of Peter, in the Catholic Church.

As Pope Saint John Paul II said in the first sentence of his introduction to the *Catechism of the Catholic Church*, "Guarding the Deposit of Faith is the mission which the Lord entrusted to His Church, and which she fulfills in every age."[45] He also once said:

> Offering himself freely in his passion and death on the cross, the Son of God took upon himself all the evil of sin. The suffering of the crucified God is not just one form of suffering alongside others, not just another more or less painful ordeal; it is an unequaled suffering. In sacrificing himself for us all, Christ gave a new meaning to suffering, opening up a new dimension, a new order of love.[46]

One of the main things I've tried to admit in writing this book is that I don't think—in my blind acceptance and active embrace of our modern industrial, progressivist culture—that I would have discovered the authentic call to gospel simplicity if I hadn't moved from the din of the city out to the demanding peace of our rural land.

In like manner, I don't think I would have *heard* the full truth of the gospel in my Protestant Evangelicalism, as good as it was. What I preached was true as far as it went, but it had been channeled down a potentially myopic dead end, through the Reformers' obsession with self-actualization. By reducing the gospel to faith *alone*, they truncated Christianity to *being* in Christ, essentially stopping spiritual growth at the beginning and removed any necessity for *abiding* and *loving* in Christ. Faith *alone* in Jesus blinded me to the more important and central issues of the gospel, and I never saw the need to dig deeper, due to the assumptions of "imputed righteousness" and "once saved, always saved." Through their devotion to Christ, sincere Bible-believing Christians hear the true call of the gospel, but dangerously, by not seeing the signal importance of *abiding* and the call to detached, humble *love*, they may not in the end attain intimacy with Christ.

Yet history demonstrates all too often how Catholics, from the pope on down to the lowliest layman, have also failed to live out the gospel, for Catholics can too often miss the point of their Catholicism. The point is not ritual or structure or triumphantly preserving the history, the saints, the sacraments, the devotions, or ecclesial authority. All of these, including faith in Christ *alone*, are to equip us to fulfill the great commandments to love. The saving grace of the Eucharist, as Catholics say "amen" in their reception of the Body and Blood of Christ—as Christ demanded of His followers if they desire to "have eternal life" (see Jn 6:51–58)—is not merely the faithful partaking of it as Catholics, but the surrendering self-identification of one's union with the self-sacrifice of Christ for others: partaking is a vow of obedience to go and do likewise, to imitate Christ—to become by grace a "living sacrifice" (see Rom 12:1).

This is reiterated repeatedly in the devotional classic by Thomas à Kempis that has been declared by both Catholics and Protestants as likely the most popular book in history, next to the Scriptures:

> Of what use is it to discourse learnedly on the Trinity, if you lack humility and therefore displease the Trinity? Lofty words do not make a man just or holy; but a good life makes him dear to God. I would far rather feel contrition than be able to define it. If you knew the whole Bible by heart, and all the teachings of the philosophers, how would this help you without the grace and love of God? "Vanity of vanities, and all is vanity," except to love God and serve Him alone. And this is supreme wisdom—to despise the world, and draw daily nearer to the kingdom of heaven.[47]

This is why I am glad to be a Catholic: not so I can somehow rest assured of salvation since I have come to know that Christ established the Church as "necessary for salvation" and consequently have "come home"; rather, it is because, by grace, I have come to realize that, in the arrogant, proud, self-assured, and independently concocted interpretation of biblical Christianity that I proclaimed from my Presbyterian pulpit, I likely would not have learned how to abide in Christ and especially how to love—and not received the necessary sacramental graces to do so, unless I had come home to the Church.

For this and many, many other reasons, Marilyn and I are glad to be home.

If, by chance, you have even a tweak of a leaning toward at least considering the Catholic Faith, I'd like to invite you to consider connecting to the website for the *Coming Home Network International.* Certainly, I encourage you to contact your local Catholic parish, if you feel comfortable doing that, but frankly, this is not always easy or beneficial. But please be assured, from its inception more than thirty years ago, the *Coming Home Network* has been committed never to "push, pull, or prod" anyone into the Catholic Church; they are committed to standing beside anyone who inquires. At the website (www.chnetwork.org) you will find many free resources, an online community, and especially lots of stories about how people, through grace and the leading of the Holy Spirit, were drawn to a deeper relationship with Christ and His Church.

Appendix 2

Radical Financial Planning

I'm hesitant to do this—because I recognize I am not a qualified financial advisor—but I would suggest that the teachings of Saint Thomas Aquinas, as summarized by Bishop George Speltz, establish a workable guideline for planning for our economic future (discussed earlier in chapter 6, beginning page 54). A banker once asked me what I thought my wife and I would need annually to support ourselves after I "retire" (whatever that is). $50,000? $100,000? A gazillion? I had no clue how to respond, admittedly because (having not yet done any of the things recommended in this book), our life together was already overflowing with unnecessary stuff, the constant maintenance of it, and the presumed goal of accumulating more.

Using the advice of Aquinas and Bishop Speltz, however, provides a much more workable approach. Let me begin by suggesting that the question "What will you or your family need for the future?" is not the right question. Besides the fact that, for many reasons, the question is unanswerable, it also blindly presumes the individualism of our modern culture. It is not merely what I, or my wife and I, or my family and I will need but what we will need within the community in which we live, or plan to live, or maybe need to live. In the same way that the salvation of our souls was never intended to be an individualistic matter but rather a matter of living as faithful individuals within the community or People of God, so we were created to live within extended communities, in which we help provide for each other's needs. This is the core of subsidiarity: what we cannot provide for ourselves, our immediate community can and should provide. Therefore, it's not merely about providing enough investments in stocks and bonds to gamble that the eventual profits will provide enough capital for our individual needs; rather, we must look to the community in which we have chosen to live out the rest of our lives as the source for our shared needs.

The first and most essential things for which we will need to plan are those things that, according to Aquinas and Speltz, provide for our bodily and spiritual needs:

- air
- food
- water
- clothing
- shelter
- spiritual nourishment

Air was taken for granted in Aquinas' day, but not so in ours. Some of us live in polluted environments that, for the sake of our health and that of our children, we may need to leave. And spiritual nourishment, both through private devotions as well as the gathered local community of the Church and her sacraments, is not a mere add-on but is as essential to our well-being as the other bodily goods. To deny this is to blindly starve ourselves spiritually into oblivion.

So, making a checklist, how will you and your community provide for these bodily goods? Can you grow all or most of your food, or will you need to buy it locally? If the latter, you will need a source of income or sufficient savings. Do you have a natural source of water, or will you need to buy this from the community? Do you have sufficient clothing to last you until you die, or will you need to replenish your wardrobe? Are you mortgaged to the hilt, renting, or do you own your home outright? Can you heat your home with wood from your land, or will you need to pay utilities? Can you walk to church, or will you need assistance in getting there? And in today's world, I should add this: Will you and family be equipped to handle all of the waste and refuse on your property, or will you need to pay someone to haul it away?

These are some key questions for discerning your future needs, for there are many people who spend their twilight years with only these things. For some, this will be out of necessity: in bed due to disability, receiving oxygen artificially, food and fluids intravenously, adequate bedclothes, minimal but sufficient shelter, and a visiting minister or priest. Others, however, accept this simplicity by choice: a simple home without any major debts, wearing basic but modest clothing, a garden and full pantry, a well or cistern, a composting system, and an easy walk to church. In either case, though, with only these minimal bodily goods, a person can live for many years—and with the right heart, can live in contentment.

Beyond these more traditional bodily goods, today we must also consider:

- transportation
- communication

When we humans lived in smaller, self-sufficient communities, both transportation and communication were less significant issues. We could procure most of what we needed on foot or horseback, and we could yell across the pasture or ride to a neighbor for conversation. But as transportation and communication technologies advanced and reshaped our world, our lives and communities became so transformed that it has become next to impossible for most of us to live without cars, cell phones, email, the Internet, and even social networking. As we plan for the future, we need to discern how essential these technologies will be for our lives, for each will require more and more outflow of money to power, upgrade, and repair. The more we can simplify our lives, enhancing and developing the sustaining benefits of our local communities, the simpler will be the demands on our future resources and plans.

There is another obviously important issue I've left out of this list:

- health care

Should this be included in the first category as an essential bodily need—a right that every individual has for the well-being of his whole person, and therefore the well-being of his soul? Of all the issues, this has become the most complicated, as well as political. How much health care do we need? What criteria do we use to determine how much health care is necessary or extravagant? The rise of the health-care industry has exactly paralleled the rise of the industrial revolution. Driven by the altruistic goals of alleviating all suffering and pain, as well as extending life at whatever cost, coupled with the limitless potential of greed in our free-market culture, health care has risen, in the minds of Americans, to the top of the list of essential bodily goods.

Given the fact that none of the leaders of our country or our government, or the leaders of our churches, can agree on the best approach to providing fair and adequate health care, I won't presume to know the answer. However, it seems to me that the answer needs to be a personal one: the more we expect the government to take care of us, the less free we may become to follow God and His radical call to detachment.

I also believe that this requires a rethinking of the place of suffering in our lives. The escalation of modern health care is built upon the presumption that it is always good to alleviate pain and suffering and to extend life as long as possible. Voluntary fasting has long been recommended as a practical spiritual discipline that prepares us—body and soul, intellect and will—to face larger trials, through a long period of lesser deprivations. Is it not possible that the lesser sufferings of most of our lives are given by God as preparation for facing the larger and potentially longer sufferings of our later years?

It's a personal decision, of course, but the more we can accept suffering as a regular, even positive, aspect of life, the less our lives will be subject to the politics and economics of our troubled health-care system. As the Apostle Paul reminded his Christian audience in Rome:

> We are children of God, and if children, then heirs, heirs of God and fellow heirs with Christ, provided we suffer with him in order that we may also be glorified with him. (Rom 8:16-17)

I realize this call to accept suffering is hard to stomach (and it's especially easier to write about "the call to accept suffering" when one's life is relatively free from suffering, as mine mostly is, by the mercy of God). This is why modern evangelists find it much easier to fill basketball-arena-sized worship centers by preaching a comfort-laden "health and wealth" gospel than the gospel of Christ, who said, "Deny yourself, take up your cross, and follow me" (see Mt 16:24). Thomas à Kempis always seems to say it best:

> Be assured of this, that you must live a dying life. And the more completely a man dies to self, the more he begins to live to God. No man is fit to understand heavenly things, unless he is resigned to bear hardships for Christ's sake. Nothing is more acceptable to God, and nothing more salutary for yourself, than to suffer gladly for Christ's sake. And if it lies in your choice, you should choose rather to suffer hardships for Christ's sake, than to be refreshed by many consolations; for thus you will more closely resemble Christ and all His Saints. For our merit and spiritual progress does not consist in enjoying such sweetness and consolation, but rather in the bearing of great burdens and troubles.

Yet, once these basic bodily goods have been provided, there are other secondary yet necessary goods: for what are we to do with ourselves once the cupboards, refrigerator, cistern, and closets in our simple home are full? Herein lie our vocations: What are we to do with the gifts, talents, and opportunities God has provided in the unique places in which He has "exiled" us? These secondary yet essential goods are:

- work
- service
- leisure

This surely needs a much longer and more philosophical discussion, but to put it simply, we each were created to share in God's work. For the underlying goal of fulfilling our created purpose, He called us to use our time and talents productively for ends that are good, true, and beautiful. This requires prayerful discernment as well as guidance from those we trust within our religious community. To follow Aquinas' advice, however, working to provide directly for the bodily needs of our family—the work of a husbandman—is a good and holy vocation. To what extent can we dedicate our working days to providing for the bodily goods of our families? What we can't grow or make, we will need to buy. To the extent that the vocation to which we are called prevents us from growing or making, we will need to provide more money to buy, preferably supporting those in our local community. This was the key to the success of the traditional, self-sustaining communities that built our nation and our world, where each person had a working place within the community. No one starved, no one was naked or homeless, and no one was unemployed, if they desired to work.

But we have pretty much lost this self-sustaining world—except in small pockets, such as the Amish communities (though even these are becoming less self-sustaining). Most of us have long since abandoned the agrarian world, following careers that not only make it hard to find time to garden or remodel our homes but have prevented us from learning these skills or developing the necessary muscles.

Yet, if we look to a simpler future for ourselves and our families, it becomes more feasible to reconsider how we will focus our work as we grow older. If we are intent on "living in the lifestyle to which we have become accustomed," overflowing with unnecessary things that have no natural limit, and especially with those addictive technologies that always require more and more costly energy, updates, syncing, et cetera, then we will have no choice except to work more and more hours, and sink more and more money into investments run by people we will never see and whose values we will never know. On the other hand, the more we can shift our work to directly providing these bodily goods, through gardening or even farming on one's own unmortgaged land, and developing interdependent relationships with our neighbors and local farmers, the less our futures will be affected by the whims of our culture.

Next to work, service is the greatest task we can do with our time and talents. Once we have provided for the needs of spouse and family, how can we reach out to help those around us, especially the less fortunate? So many thousands of people retire only to focus on themselves, either on their leisure or in spending years in front of a television watching reruns of *The Golden Girls*. It would take only a little effort, however, to find ways to give of ourselves as volunteers, and in doing so, we might find that through the joy that comes from giving, we may want little beyond our basic bodily goods to find happiness and contentment.

And once our work and service are done for the day, leisure is a good gift of God's overflowing joy. This can include reading, exercise, music, games, and, yes, even television, but especially hobbies. Hobbies are a great way of experiencing the creative energy of God and can feed a vein of contentment and gratitude that can change an otherwise discouraged, lonely life into one of joyful giving and camaraderie.

Finally, two more items that are essential to the list:

- paying yourself
- paying God

Some money managers emphasize the need to pay yourself first, setting aside ten percent or more of savings before anything else. This is certainly an admirable goal, but where should this fit in the above list? I would suggest that providing the basic bodily needs for one's family should always come first, because bodily goods enable the whole person, body and soul, to grow in virtue, happiness, and, consequently, contentment. Setting aside savings for the future, especially to cover the certain occurrence of emergencies, should then precede the accumulation of all lesser external goods, and for the primary purpose of providing future bodily goods. Since there is no limit to the amount of external goods we may eventually want or think we "need," there is no way to determine how many gazillions we might need to save.

Paying God, however, through donations to church or other charities, I believe, should take precedence before anything else on the list. The example of the widow's mite (Lk 21:1-4) sets the standard. Before we even provide for the basic bodily essentials, we should learn the practice of setting aside (i.e., letting go of) even a small portion of what God has provided for us. This becomes a regular, active expression of trust in God's providence—for He's really the only one who knows what we and our families will need for the future.

On the other hand, adopting the strategy of paying yourself first can become a regular, active, deceiving habit of trusting the future to ourselves, our accumulation, the presumed progress of our culture, the assured rebound of our economy, and the foresight of financial analysts. As I was writing this, a report was released by a top economist that "the average 401(k) plan grew by $11,000 from 2021 to 2024, but when adjusted for inflation, it represents a $12,000 (9.2%) loss! Researchers found that retirement plan balances also increased by nearly $30 trillion by the third quarter of 2024. But after adjusting for inflation, the retirement plans are worth roughly $27 trillion, [which amounts to] a $2.5 trillion real loss."

Beginning with small donations, as we are able to provide more for the basic needs of our families, we can increase our giving to God, which has the amazing way of instilling that "peace of God, which passes all understanding" (Phil 4:7).

The above suggestions can be itemized to form the basis for a future fiscal plan, but it will require a willingness to trust and to share. I'm certainly not suggesting that everyone is called to reduce their investments down to these minimums, but the exercise of comparing these basic minimums with how we have presently invested our money can be enlightening and can challenge us to examine why we may not be experiencing the level of contentment we had hoped we might, especially as we enter the final years of our lives.

Endnotes

1 *The Spiritual Exercises of Saint Ignatius: A New Translation* by Thomas Corbishley, S.J. (New York: P.J. Kenedy & Sons, 1963), 108.

2 Ibid.

3 The modifications to the text are from my own exegetical translation of the Hebrew text.

4 Here are the commands that Saints Peter and Paul address directly to wives. As you read, you can clearly see why I'm hesitant to say anything in an exhortative posture to you wives, given the myriad views of marriage and relationships running rampant in our post-Christian world, as well as our varied Christian communities. Even our Church leaders are sheepish about these verses! But I'll just remind us that these are quotes from Scripture written by the two most revered founding fathers of the early Church, and, as far as I know, there has never been anything in the official teaching of the Church to modify or negate these unapologetic commands of Saints Peter and Paul:

> Be subject to one another out of reverence for Christ. Wives, be subject to your husbands, as to the Lord. For the husband is the head of the wife as Christ is the head of the church, his body, and is himself its Savior. As the church is subject to Christ, so let wives also be subject in everything to their husbands. … And let the wife see that she respects her husband. (Eph 5:21-24, 33b)

> Likewise you wives, be submissive to your husbands, so that some, though they do not obey the word, may be won without a word by the behavior of their wives, when they see your reverent and chaste behavior. Let not yours be the outward adorning with braiding of hair, decoration of gold, and wearing of fine clothing, but let it be the hidden

person of the heart with the imperishable jewel of a gentle and quiet spirit, which in God's sight is very precious. So once the holy women who hoped in God used to adorn themselves and were submissive to their husbands, as Sarah obeyed Abraham, calling him lord. And you are now her children if you do right and let nothing terrify you. (1 Peter 3:1-6)

5 *Catechism of the Catholic Church*, para. 1605.

6 Quoted in Paul Bois, "'Dune' Director Denis Villeneuve: 'Human Beings Are Ruled by Algorithms Right Now … Society Is Crumbling,'|" Breitbart, December 28, 2024, https://www.breitbart.com/entertainment/2024/12/28/denis-villeneuve-human-beings-ruled-by-algorithms/.

7 Irenaeus, *Against Heresies*, trans. the Rev. John Keble (Oxford: James Parker, 1872), 113-114, emphasis mine.

8 John O'Brien, *Roads to Rome* (London: W.H. Allen, 1955), 16.

9 Ibid.

10 Ibid, 19-20.

11 Quoted in Paul Elie, *The Life You Save May Be Your Own* (New York: Farrar, Straus & Giroux, 2003), 117.

12 E.F. Schumacher, *Small Is Beautiful* (1973; reprint, New York: Harper Perennial, 2010). Also, see Joseph Pearce's insightful review and reflection on this book, *Small Is Still Beautiful: Economics as if Families Mattered* (Wilmington, DE: Intercollegiate Studies Institute, 2006).

13 E.F. Schumacher, "Technology & Political Change," in *This I Believe and Other Essays* (Devon, U.K.: Resurgence Books, 1998), 98–99.

14 Ibid., 100.

15 George H. Speltz, *The Importance of the Rural Life, According to the Philosophy of Saint Thomas Aquinas* (1944; reissue, Lexington: Saint Pius X Press, 2011).

16 Ibid., 3-4.

17 Ibid., 5.

18 Ibid., 5–6, modification mine.

19 Ibid., 6.

20 Hank Williams, Sr., "House of Gold," Sony/ATV Music Publishing LLC, Warner/Chappell Music, Inc.

21 Words by Joe Young & Sam M. Lewis, music by Walter Donaldson (New York: Waterson, Berlin & Snyder Co., Music Publishing, 1919).

22 Dr. Tobias Lanz, *Flee to the Fields: The Faith and Works of the Catholic Land Movement* (Norfolk, VA: IHS Press, 2003), 8.

23 David Mallett, "Garden Song", BMG Music, Cherry Lane Music Publishing Company.

24 From the US Debt Clock.org, at usdebtclock.org.

25 Rick Moran, "Gates: Software to Replace Millions of Human Jobs in 20 Years," in *The American Thinker*, March 15, 2014, http://www.americanthinker.com/blog/2014/03/gates_software_to_replace_millions_of_human_jobs_in_20_years.html.

26 Kevin J. Jones, "LGBT Activist Group Hopes to Influence Family Synod," Catholic News Agency, October 15, 2014, https://www.catholicnewsagency.com/news/30719/lgbt-activist-group-hopes-to-influence-family-synod.

27 Marcus Grodi, "Inch by Inch, Row by Row: A Reflection on the Beatitudes as a Staircase of Conversion," Coming Home Newtwork International, September 10, 2014, https://chnetwork.org/2014/09/10/inch-inch-row-row/.

28 Pope Saint Leo the Great, Sermon 95, A Homily on the Beatitudes, quoted in *The Liturgy of the Hours*, vol. 4, 22nd Week, Thursday, Office of Readings, 207.

29 Pope Saint Leo the Great, Sermon 95.

30 Thomas à Kempis, *The Imitation of Christ* (New York: Penguin Books, 1982), 57, 58.

31 William F. Arndt and F. Wilbur Gingrich, *A Greek-English Lexicon of the New Testament* (Chicago: University of Chicago Press, 1957), 510.

32 Ibid., 753.

33 From "Old Rivers," by Cliff Richards, 1962.

34 Thomas Merton, *The Seven Storey Mountain* (Orlando: Harcourt, 1990), 409.

35 Kempis, *The Imitation of Christ*, p. 43.

36 St. Francis, from a letter written to all the faithful, in *Opuscula*, ed. Quaracchi (1949), 87–94, quoted in *The Liturgy of the Hours*, vol. 4, Office of Readings for October 4, Feast of St. Francis of Assisi.

37 Réginald Garrigou-Lagrange, O.P., *Three Ways of the Spiritual Life* (Rockford, IL: TAN Books, 1977), 30.

38 C.S. Lewis to Arthur Greeves, December 20, 1943, in *Yours, Jack: Spiritual Direction from C.S. Lewis* (New York: HarperCollins, 2008), 97–98.

39 Marcus Grodi, *Life from Our Land* (San Francisco: Ignatius Press, 2015).

40 Steve Nicholls, *Paradise Found* (Chicago: University of Chicago Press, 2009), 427.

41 David B. Barrett, George T. Kurian, and Todd M. Johnson, eds., *World Christian Encyclopedia: A Comparative Survey of Churches and Religions in the Modern World*, vol. I (New York: Oxford University Press, 2001), 18.

42 A more detailed account of our journey into the Catholic Church can be found in *Journeys Home*, 3rd ed. (Zanesville, OH: Coming Home Resources, 2011).

43 Quoted in Kenneth J. Howell, *Clement of Rome & the Didache* (Zanesville, OH: Coming Home Resources, 2012), 115.

44 Saint Irenaeus, *Against Heresies*, 3.2.2.

45 Apostolic Constitution *Fidei Depositum: On the Publication of the Catechism of the Catholic Church* (October 11, 1992), in *Catechism of the Catholic Church*, 2nd ed. (Vatican City: Libreria Editrice Vaticana, 1997), 1.

46 Pope John Paul II, *Memory and Identity: Conversations at the Dawn of a Millennium* (New York: Rizzoli, 2005).

47 Kempis, *The Imitation of Christ*, 27–28.

ABOUT THE AUTHOR

Marcus Grodi is a husband, father, grandfather, lousy farmer, and former pastor and engineer, appeared on television and radio, and does a little bit of writing and public speaking.

Marcus received a bachelor of science degree from Case Institute of Technology (CWRU) in Polymer Engineering and a master of divinity degree from Gordon-Conwell Theological Seminary. He worked for six years as an engineer and for more than forty-five years in some form of Christian ministry. He served as the Founder and President of The Coming Home Network International and hosted *The Journey Home* television program and the *Deep in Scripture* radio program, both on EWTN. His articles have appeared in many publications and online sources. He is the author or editor of ten books, including, most recently, *Guideposts for the Journey Home*, by EWTN. Marcus has taught college and graduate courses in youth ministry, leadership, catechetics, and theology. He and his wife, Marilyn, are now empty-nesters on their thirty-eight-acre cottage farm in central Ohio.